Ideas in the Workplace

Ideas in the Workplace

Planning for Protection

H. Clarke Anawalt

CAROLINA
ACADEMIC
PRESS

IDEAS IN THE WORKPLACE

Carolina Academic Press
P.O. Box 51879
Durham, North Carolina 27717

LC Number 86-72658
ISBN 0-89089-315-2

Printed in the United States of America

Jacket and text design by C. Mayapriya Long

Contents

Acknowledgements

I want to thank the following people who have been very helpful to me in preparation of this book: Susan Anawalt for her ideas on people's practical problems and for careful criticism of sections of the writing; Betty Carlson for her excellent work preparing the manuscript; Elizabeth Enayati, Rebecca Thompson, Esq. and Debra Bartle Bristow, Esq. for research; Sheryl Heckmann, Esq. for research and editorial assistance in the final revision; and John R. Eastling for bringing together a very helpful panel of attorneys to consider "high tech" problems. The panel members were John Eastling, Marshall Phelps, Jr., Richard H. Stern, Richard L. Bernacchi, Daniel W. Vittum Jr., and myself. I have also had the benefit of working through practical problems with other attorneys, with technology workers, and with students in the Computer Law Class at the Santa Clara University Law School.

Ideas in the Workplace

CHAPTER **1**

Employer and Employee Claims to Ideas

Today, ideas and hard work create many valuable new products and processes. This is especially noticeable in the related fields of computers and telecommunications. The environment for producing new technology is "education intensive and capital intensive."[1] The development of sound ideas into useful processes and products is dependent on a cooperative and comfortable work environment. The working environments are generally provided by companies or partnerships formed in order to advance technology and serve new markets. In short, most "idea workers" work for companies.

It should be stressed that, for the most part, employers and employees work cooperatively to achieve their business objectives. To a certain degree, this book ignores the aspect of cooperation that exists in the employment relationship. Instead, it focuses on an important fissure between the employer and the employee. There is a natural tension which is created or fostered by the very process of developing and producing new items. Both the employer and the employee want to benefit from new discoveries and applications. The value of new developments may cause the previously cooperating partners to divide and quarrel.

The purpose of this book is to determine the relative rights of the employer and the employee to ideas and processes which are developed during the period of employment.

Who owns ideas?

No one "owns" ideas. Ownership is a legal concept which indicates that one has a claim of right or of property to a certain matter. As a general proposition, you simply cannot "own" an idea. You can keep an idea to yourself and prevent others from using or enjoying it. You can also develop an idea (alone or in conjunction with others) into a method or product that

---

1. A comment made by John Eastling, attorney at law, at the meeting of The Task Force on Legal Aspects of Computer Based Technology, January 1984.

you ultimately share with others. However, the *process* of the development of ideas and the materials or products developed may be legally protected. Thus, while no one really owns ideas, the products of ideas may be owned and protected by law.[2]

A good work environment

At the outset it is important to note certain characteristics of a productive working environment. One object of the rules and procedures which we will consider should be to preserve such an environment. A good working environment for high technology development should include the following:

1. Freedom of inquiry on the part of the individual
2. Mutual trust among colleagues
3. Access to information
4. A safe and healthful place to work
5. Comfortable physical surroundings
6. Encouragement for good work
7. Confidence or reliability on the part of co-workers
8. Honesty and integrity on the part of workers and supervisors
9. Quality working materials and tools of the trade
10. Protection of confidential information

These factors combine to form an environment conducive to productivity. Achievement of such an environment is the responsibility of the employer and the employee alike.

The employee who wants to leave

Any employment arrangement or contract should be founded on the assumption that a smooth working relationship will be achieved. This, however, is not always the case. Various things may jar a smooth working relationship. On the part of the employee there may be problems with cheating, unnecessary absences, or poor or lazy performance. On the part of the employer there may be such actions as unrealistic demands, poor physical conditions, discriminatory actions, invasions of privacy, or dis-

---

2. See *Protection of Computer Idea Work Today and Tomorrow*, IEEE SOFTWARE, Volume 1, No. 2, April 1984. The definition and the means of protecting intellectual property are explained in chapter 2. *See also* the section on implied terms in the employment contract in chapter 3 for limited instances where one may speak of ownership of ideas.

respect. Any of these phenomena can begin to dissolve a healthy working relationship.

Let us assume, though, that there is an entirely satisfactory working relationship between employer and employee at the outset. This arrangement can be shaken or changed by new factors and changed circumstances. The employee may see new opportunities, want greater ego satisfaction, see his or her life wasting away, or find new markets for his or her skills. These things may cause the employee to become restive and seek new, more rewarding employment or self-employment. The employer, on the other hand, may also see new opportunities, may demand a higher level of performance from the employee, tie up more of the employee's intellectual work product, or use the employee in new endeavors. These changing factors in the environment are not "negative" in the same way as cheating or discrimination. Rather, they are natural progressions of the process of growing and learning in a changing technical environment. It is when these factors start to predominate in the employment relationship that practical problems and legal problems may arise.

Let us consider a typical situation: An employee is well educated in his technical field of knowledge. He has always wanted to strike out on his own and make the most of his talents and efforts. Another employer offers him a better salary and benefits. Or perhaps a group of colleagues decide to go out on their own and set up a venture. Time is ripe for him. His productive capacity could not be better, and he is jam-packed with ideas. He decides to leave.

Who owns the idea work products?

The employee may leave or may wish to develop a profitable enterprise alongside his or her current job. In either case, a definite *legal* question is raised. Who owns or has the right to use the idea work products developed during the period of employment? The answer will differ from individual case to individual case.

Let us suppose that Ms. Jones, an employee for Audio Dynamics, has developed a superior hearing aid which relies on a built-in mini computer.[3] The new hearing aid was developed while she worked for Audio Dynamics, which is a manufacturer of stereo components. Whether she or the employer owns (or has the right to use) the new development will depend on answers to questions such as:

1. Who thought up the idea and developed it?

---

3. Both Ms. Jones and Audio Dynamics are fictional characters. Any similarity to any existing individual or company is purely coincidental.

2. Where and when was the design perfected?
3. Does Ms. Jones have an employment contract? If so, what does it provide?
4. Does the hearing aid design rely on patents, copyrights, or trade secrets of Audio Dynamics?
5. Has she disclosed her work to her employer?

The legal answers to a situation such as this will depend on law drawn from fields of patent, copyright, trade secrets, employment contracts, antitrust, and shop rights, as well as the specific provisions of *her* employment contract.

People in a variety of different fields produce valuable idea work products. The possibilities for these idea products are probably limitless. Consider some examples drawn from cases discussed in this book:

- computer screening of seismic activity
- methods for training pilots
- mathematical control of rubber curing
- video game shows
- computer operating systems
- computer graphics processes
- plain paper copiers
- cartoons
- manufacturing processes
- television quiz show formats

Each of these idea products has a value, and the innovator in each case should enjoy some recognition and compensation for his or her efforts. This book sets forth legal doctrines and practical approaches for determining claims to ideas in the workplace.

CHAPTER 2

Intellectual Property

Basic premises of intellectual property law

It is important that the inventor and his or her lawyer have a working understanding of the law of intellectual property. Certain intellectual work products are protectable by law; others are not. Even that which can be protected by law may not be.

The "law of ideas" is quite interesting. Before we plunge directly into the specific categories of intellectual property law, it is well to observe some basic propositions:

1. ***No one owns ideas.*** Ideas in themselves are not subject to individual ownership or control. Ideas are like the air we breathe— available to all. The United States Supreme Court has stated that "an idea of itself is not patentable."[1] Copyright law explicitly rejects copyright of an idea.[2]

2. ***Legal protection of inventions, processes, and expressions is established for the good of the public.*** "In order to reap the benefits of new technology, society depends both on encouragement of the innovators and on the dissemination of ideas."[3] The basic approach in our legal system is that the rewards provided to inventors are established in order to advance the public interest. The rewards to inventors are a means to this end, not ends in themselves.

   "The copyright law, like the patent statutes, makes reward to the owner a secondary consideration . . . The economic philosophy behind the clause empowering Congress to grant patents and copyrights is the conviction that encouragement of individual effort by

---

1. Gottschalk v. Benson, 409 U.S. 63, 67, 93 S.Ct. 253, 255 (1972) (quoting Rubber-Tip Pencil Co. v. Howard, 20 Wall (87 U.S. 498, 507, 22 L.Ed. 410).
2. 17 U.S.C. Section 102(b) (1982). See pages 28–30 and 54–58 for limited ways in which ownership of ideas may be claimed by contract.
3. Task Force on Legal Aspects of Computer Based Technology, *Protection of Computer Ideawork Today and Tomorrow*, IEEE SOFTWARE, April 1984, at 74.

personal gain is the best way to advance public welfare through the talents of authors and inventors . . . "[4]

Protection of intellectual property is thus dependent on legislative and judicial recognition of the balance between the needs of invention and the interest of idea dissemination. Legal and practical resolutions of ownership questions in the area of intellectual work are never far removed from these basic principles. The inventor must understand what can be protected under these laws so that he or she can have reasonable expectations of protection and know how to achieve those expectations.

Basic forms of intellectual property

An intellectual work product may be protected by law, and when it is, it is usually referred to as "intellectual property." American law recognizes three basic forms of intellectual property protection mechanisms—patent, copyright, and trade secret. Patent law is based entirely on federal patent statutes, 35 U.S.C. Section 1 and following. Generally it protects inventions that are embodied in some physical process. Copyright law is also based on a federal statute, the Copyright Act of 1976. Federal patent and copyright laws preempt their respective fields and preclude contrary state laws.[5]

Trade secret law is common law which has developed to protect valuable ideas and applications which would otherwise not be protected. Because of its common law origin, it is likely to vary from state to state, although it is safe to say that the different states draw on each other's law and there is much uniformity.[6] It is, as we shall see, primarily a way of protecting ideas through active vigilance and self-help. Trade secret law is just what it indicates—a recognition that some things are secret.[7]

Patent

**Patent law—
ownership
of use rights**

Patent law is the "traditional" law for protecting inventions. A utility patent gives an inventor the right to exclude all others from making, using,

---

4. Mazer v. Stein, 347 U.S. 201, 219, 74 S.Ct. 460, 471 (1954), (quoting United States v. Paramount Pictures, 334 U.S. 131, 158 [1948]).

5. Sears Roebuck and Co. v. Stiffel Co., 376 U.S. 225 (1964), Kewanee Oil Co. v. Bicron Corp., 416 U.S. 470 (1974), and 17 U.S.C. Section 301.

6. A widely followed definition of trade secret is set forth in Comment B to Section 757 of the Restatement (First) of Torts: "any formula, pattern, device or compilation of information which is used in one's business, and which gives him an opportunity to obtain an advantage over competitors who do not know or use it." Some states have enacted the Uniform Trade Secrets Act. *See*, for example, Minnesota Statutes Annotated, Section 325C.01 et seq. set forth in the Appendix.

7. The Appendix contains a bibliography of other useful references.

or selling his or her inventions for seventeen years as a reward for creation of a product or process that is useful to the public at large.[8] The patent owner has an exclusive right to the use of the patented process even against those who use the process unintentionally, or who appear to have created the process independently.[9] The quid pro quo for this property right is full disclosure of the patent process and dedication of the process to the public after the expiration of the patent.[10]

The value of use rights can be demonstrated by the phenomenal business success of Xerox Corporation. That company realized billions of dollars of revenue from a single invention, the plain paper copier, between 1960 and 1970 when it enjoyed a complete monopoly of the process. The monopoly was made possible and assured by the patent involved, and the patent even insulated the company from certain antitrust claims.[11] This example can be repeated as to any new computer or other high tech invention which is successfully patented.

The patent issuance process

Obtaining a patent is far from automatic. It requires preparation of a carefully drawn application and ultimate approval by the patent office.[12] The work of conducting a patent search and preparing an application demands specialization and expertise. Only attorneys admitted to the patent bar are permitted to represent clients in patent proceedings.[13] The choice of whether to use patent law as a means of protecting intellectual work, however, demands broad understanding of the legal and practical considerations related to the particular invention. It is appropriate to seek advice on this decision from a wide range of informed persons. Lawyers who are not necessarily patent bar members but who have experience in the "high-tech" field may be among the best sources of legal advice today, as they should certainly be aware of the need to consult patent specialists on questions of expertise and will refer the case for patent processing as appropriate.

Much of the intellectual property being developed today in the computer area is not readily protectable by patent law. For example, copyright and

---

8. 35 U.S.C. Sections 154 and 271; Coakwell v. United States, 372 F.2d 508, 509 (1967); the patent period for a design patent is 14 years, which is available for ornamental features. 35 U.S.C. 171–173. *See* D. S. Chisum, *Patents*, sections 1.01–1.04.

9. Blair v. Westinghouse Corp., 291 F. Supp. 664, 670 (D.D.C., 1968) and Smith v. Snow, 294 U.S. 1 (1935).

10. Kewanee Oil Co. v. Bicron Corp., 416 U.S. 470, 480 (1974).

11. SCM Corp. v. Xerox Corp., 645 F.2d 1195 (1981), cert. denied 455 U.S. 1016 (1982).

12. 35 U.S.C. Sections 111–113 and 151.

13. 35 U.S.C. Sections 31–33, and Jones v. Raymond Lee Org. Inc., 209 U.S.P.Q. (BNA) 209 (C.D.Cal. 1979).

trade secret protection offer more effective means of protecting most software developments. Legal considerations, marketing concerns, and above all, the fast pace of development may militate against the choice of patent law, for it remains a slow and expensive route which requires disclosure of the secret that needs protection.[14]

Who may own a patent?

Basically anyone may own a patent. What is required is that one invent something and succeed in perfecting the patent claim.[15] Prior to the grant of a patent, the inventor has an incomplete right to his or her invention. Since the unpatented process is not protected by patent law, it may be assigned or granted to someone else.[16] Thus, either the employee as inventor or the employer as assignee of the invention rights may own a patent, although generally the inventor must first apply for the patent in his own name.[17] Ownership of patent rights which have been developed during the employment relationship will depend upon the employment contract and other factors. (Refer to pages 35–36 and 54–58.)

There is, however, a general rule followed by the courts that valuable invention rights are assumed to be retained by the inventing employee. The courts generally resist the notion that invention or patent rights are impliedly assigned to someone else. "The reluctance of courts to imply or infer an agreement by the employee to assign his patent is due to a recognition of the peculiar nature of the act of invention, which consists neither in finding out the laws of nature, nor in fruitful research as to the operation of natural laws, but in discovering of how those laws may be utilized or applied for some beneficial purpose, by a process, a device or a machine."[18]

Patentable items— new, useful, and not obvious

"Whoever invents or discovers any new and useful process, machine, manufacture, or composition of matter, or any new and useful improvement thereof, may obtain a patent therefore, subject to the conditions and requirements of this title"—35 U.S.C. Section 101. Other sections of the code clarify the substantive conditions to obtaining the patent.

One of the conditions of patentability is that the new method or process be shown to be, in fact, novel. The developer may have an approach that seems new, but is not. He or she runs into the age-old stumbling block that there is nothing new under the sun. Specifically, the federal law requires "novelty" in an objective way—that others have not already used the invention, that it was not known or used by others or disclosed before

---

14. 35 U.S.C. Section 112.
15. 15 U.S.C. Section 261.
16. Hendrie v. Sayles, 98 U.S. 546 (1879).
17. 35 U.S.C. Sections 111 and 118.
18. United States v. Dubilier Condenser Corp., 289 U.S. 178, 188 (1932).

the claimant invented it.[19] The specific definition of "novelty" is set forth in 35 U.S.C. Section 102.

Another basic condition to patentability is that the proffered method not be obvious. A development may be "novel" in the sense that no one else has used it before, yet obvious when pointed out. Such an item is not patentable. "A patent may not be obtained . . . if the differences between the subject matter sought to be patented and the prior art are such that the subject matter as a whole would have been obvious at the time the invention was made to a person having ordinary skill in the art to which said subject matter pertains."[20]

An example of obviousness is a suit which involved two large food producers. In *General Mills, Inc. v. Standard Brands, Inc.*, General Mills claimed a statutory monopoly for a method of producing fabricated "potato chips" of a uniform size and shape. Essentially the General Mills process involved towing a ribbon of preformed batter through hot oil. The result was a chain of identical saddle-shaped "potato chips" which could easily be separated, stacked, and sold in containers similar to tennis ball cans. General Mills obtained a patent covering the process. When Standard Brands produced its own chip by the process, General Mills sued for infringement. The court decided that Standard Brands was not subject to liability, as the patent was invalid. The essential element of the patent, the ribbon of dough that held the chips together, was obvious.[21] The case also illustrates another important point—the validity of a patent is subject to attack in infringement action.

A process or machine

The statutory subject matter of 35 U.S.C. Section 101 is, as we have noted, broad. Any "new and useful process" may qualify for a patent. Yet there is an important implied limit. Ideas themselves cannot be patented. Thus, if you had been the first to discover long division, you would not have been permitted to patent it under United States law. The claim stretches too far; it seeks a monopoly for all the uses of long division. If you had discovered long division, you would have been permitted only to patent a particular process or method which utilized that discovery, yet allowed it to be used in other ways. The recognition of a new idea may be an ingredient, even the critical one of the new process, but it must not preempt the use of the idea itself.

A classic modern case on this limitation is *Gottschalk v. Benson*, 409 U.S. 63 (1972). In that case the claimants Benson and Talbot had developed a method of converting binary coded decimals (BCDs) to pure binary numbers. Pure binaries are the only information that a digital computer

---

19. 35 U.S.C. Section 102 and Diamond v. Diehr, 450 U.S. 175, 189 (1981).
20. 35 U.S.C. Section 103.
21. General Mills, Inc. v. Standard Brands, Inc., 431 F. Supp. 687 (1977).

can assimilate, as their basic units "zero" and "one" can be expressed directly by the presence or absence of an electrical charge. Humans, on the other hand, get bogged down by the binary notation. As a convenience to humans, coded binary numbers are sometimes used so that humans need only recognize those binaries between zero and nine.[22] Benson's process consisted of a method of converting the coded binaries into the pure form. For this process in general, he sought a patent. He and Talbot had not restricted the claim to any particular application but presented a claim "so abstract and sweeping as to cover both known and unknown uses of the BCD to pure binary conversion."[23] The Supreme Court denied the claim. The mathematical formula could not be patented in itself.

The case of *Diamond v. Diehr*, 450 U.S. 175 (1981) also involved a claim of protection of a mathematical formula, but this time the formula was embedded in a specific rubber-molding process. Diehr's process was based on a constant recalculation of the necessary cure time for molded rubber using the continuous measurement of temperature within the mold itself. In so doing, the method *applied* a mathematical formula in a physical process. "A mathematical formula as such is not accorded the protection of our patent laws. . . . On the other hand, when a claim containing a mathematical formula implements or applies that formula in a structure or process which, when considered as a whole, is performing a function which the patent laws were designed to protect (e.g., transforming or reducing an article to a different state or thing), then the claim satisfies the requirements of Section 101."[24]

Thus, the boundaries of patent law require that a claim be limited to a *particular* process. If that process is new and useful, then it will be protected, but the general approach or algorithm will remain open to other uses.

Difficult to patent software

The rule of the preceding section can be restated: the process alone is patentable; the underlying general (mathematical) algorithm is not. This has long been the rule:

> He who discovers a hitherto unknown phenomenon of nature has no claim to a monopoly of it which the law recognizes. If there is to be invention from such a discovery, it must come from the application of the law of nature to a new and useful end.[25]

---

22. I understand that with current programming techniques coded binary numbers are not nearly so useful or important.

23. 409 U.S. at 68.

24. 450 U.S. at 191–192 (1980).

25. *Funk Brothers Seed Co. v. Kalo Inoculant Co.*, 333 U.S. 127, 130 quoted in Gottschalk v. Benson, 409 U.S. 63 at 67.

Because of the nature of computer software developments, they will more often than not fail this test.

Software developments, if they are to be patentable at all, must be new. Yet newness in this field seems most often to be the description of a different step-by-step process of handling information. Thus, the inventor is faced with Scylla and Charybdis.[26] If the step-by-step process is one easily derived from prior work in the computer field, a patent claim will be rejected because it is obvious under 35 U.S.C. Section 103. If it is not obvious, it will probably be new, because it captures a new general method or algorithm.[27] A process embodying the algorithm may be patented, but the software invention is likely to be viewed as a claim to the algorithm itself, thus violating the rule.

Software applications may be patentable under the following guidelines:

1. A mathematical algorithm may be part of the claim. The presence of such an algorithm does not invalidate the claim.
2. If a mathematical algorithm is part of the claim, the claimant must be sure that it is linked to a specific application.
3. The specific applications most likely to achieve a patent grant are those with a strong and definite link to hardware or to resolution of a physical process.[28]

The boundaries of patentability are illustrated by a comparison of two cases. In *In re Sarkar*, 588 F.2d 1330 (C.C.P.A. 1978) Sarkar sought to protect a mathematical model which was capable of accurately providing the flow parameters of a river taking into account obstructions, flooding, influence of tides, and other factors. The court rejected Sarkar's claim because, as stated, the novelty of his approach derived solely from a "disembodied" mathematical exercise. On the other hand, in *In re Johnson*, 589 F.2d 1070 (C.C.P.A. 1978) a patent was granted for a claim which bore some similarity to that of *Sarkar*. Johnson also sought a patent for a process that abstractly modeled a geophysical phenomenon, seismic activity. The critical difference appears to be that the mathematical formulas set forth in the Johnson claim were recited within the confines of a specific machine-

---

26. In Homer's *Odyssey*, Odysseus was obliged to sail his ship through a narrow channel of water. On one side was Scylla, a sea monster whose six heads fed upon creatures including passing sailors. On the other side was Charybdis, a creature who sucked the seawater and spat it out.

27. A general definition of algorithm is "a mechanical or recursive computational procedure," THE AMERICAN HERITAGE DICTIONARY. See the excellent discussion in Nelson Moskowitz, *The Metamorphosis of Software Related Invention Patentability*, 3 COMPUTER LAW JOURNAL 273, 277–278 (1982).

28. An excellent reference for additional guidance is the Moskowitz article cited in footnote 27, especially at page 315. *See In re* Freeman, 573 F.2d 1237 (C.C.P.A. 1978); *In re* Walter, 618 F.2d 758 (C.C.P.A. 1980).

implemented process which eliminated unwanted noise from actual seismic data readings. The "close link to hardware" was the key.

In sum, the requirement of embodiment in a process makes patent an unworkable choice for protecting software in most instances. Most choices to seek patent protection should be based on a demonstrably close connection to the related hardware or physical application.[29]

Patent infringement

A patent grant is a potent means of protecting intellectual effort. Nevertheless, one must recognize that it is not a clear assurance of protection, but rather a "ticket to a lawsuit." This is because of the following practical matters:

1. Validity subject to challenge
"A patent shall be presumed valid." 35 U.S.C. Section 282. However, this presumption is subject to rebuttal. The presumption can be overcome by showing grounds of invalidity such as obviousness (*Parker v. Motorola, Inc.*, 524 F.2d 518, 521–522 [Fifth Cir., 1975]).

2. Failure of proof of infringement
The allegedly offending use may not in fact infringe (*Charles Fisher Spring Co. v. Motion Picture Screen and Accessories Co.*, 36 F. Supp. 227 [D.C.N.Y. 1940]).

3. Unexcused delay in enforcing rights
Laches or unexcused delay in enforcement of rights may defeat a claim as may other equitable defenses (*Advanced Hydraulics v. Otis Elevator*, 525 F.2d 477, 35 A.L.R. Fed 543 [Fifth Cir., 1975]).

Summary of patent law features

A patent is a statutory monopoly of use rights. It is based on a quid pro quo: the grantee makes full disclosure of his or her invention and in exchange receives the patent. A patent does not issue automatically, but must

---

29. *But see* Paine, Webber v. Merrill Lynch, Pierce, 564 F. Supp. 1358 (D. Del., 1983), in which the district court held that a method of doing business—Merrill Lynch's case management system—was patentable because it taught a method of operating a computer. This decision seems anomalous because otherwise nonstatutory subject matter cannot be made patentable merely by making it usable by a computer, and methods of doing business have long been held to be unpatentable. *See* Note, *The Patentability of Computer Programs: Merrill Lunch's Patent for a Financial Services System*, 59 IND. L.J. 633, 657 (1984); Note, *Paine, Webber, Jackson and Curtis, Inc. v. Merrill Lynch, Pierce, Fenner & Smith: Methods of Doing Business Held Patentable Because Implemented on a Computer*, 5 COMP. L. J. 101 (1984).

be granted by the patent office. It is valid for a term of seventeen years.[30] Patents are restricted to new, useful, and nonobvious creations. Software patents are very difficult to obtain. Remedies for patent infringement are broad and include injunctions and damages. In an infringement action, the patent is presumed valid, but substantial defenses are available, including claims of invalidity, failure of proof of infringement, and *laches*. Procuring and defending a patent is generally an expensive proposition.

Copyright

Copyright confers ownership of published and unpublished works of authorship which are fixed in any tangible medium of expression (17 U.S.C. Section 201). Works of authorship include seven statutory categories: literary works; musical works; dramatic works; pantomimes and choreography; pictorial, graphic and sculptural works; motion picture and other audio-visual works; and sound recordings. In addition, a 1980 amendment to the act brought computer programs under the protection of the act, not as a separate category, but as protected expressions in whatever form they may appropriately fit.[31]

The copyright law explicitly denies copyright protection of ideas per se. "In no case does copyright protection for an original work of authorship extend to any idea, procedure, process, system, method of operation, concept, principle, or discovery, regardless of the form in which it is described, explained, illustrated, or embodied in such work."[32] Thus, the key concept is protection of the *expression* of an idea. The plot of a novel may not be protected, but particular combinations of characters, language, setting, and tone may be. If *Romeo and Juliet* were protected by copyright, then *West Side Story* would not infringe it, though they are renditions of the "same story." *West Side Story*, or any other new play, is itself protectable.[33]

Protection of expression falls short of protecting general ideas, scenarios, and approaches, but it does give substantial protection to the component parts of a complete work. In other words, it does not take a word

Copyright law—
ownership of
expression

---

30. 35 U.S.C. Sections 154 and 173.

31. The effective date of the 1976 Copyright Act is January 1980. The 1980 amendments add a definition of a computer program in 17 U.S.C. Section 101: "A 'computer program' is a set of statements or instructions to be used directly or indirectly in a computer in order to bring about a certain result."

32. 17 U.S.C. Section 102(b).

33. Nichols v. Universal Pictures Corp., 45 F.2d 119 (2d Cir., 1930); Warner Brothers, Inc. v. American Broadcasting Corp., Inc., 654 F.2d 204 (2d Cir., 1981).

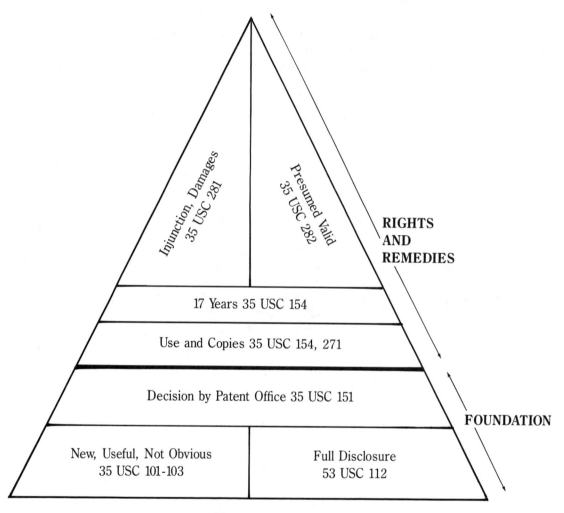

RIGHTS
AND
REMEDIES

FOUNDATION

Figure 2A
THE STRUCTURE OF PATENT PROTECTION

for word copy to constitute plagiarism. If it can be shown that another person had access to the original work and that the offending work is substantially similar, then a case of copying is made.[34]

---

34. Infringement is discussed in this chapter, pages 21–22.

The basic requirements of copyright is that the work be *fixed* in a tangible means of expression. Thus both published and unpublished works may enjoy protection once they are in some way reduced to a fixed expression. Protection of unpublished works is specifically recognized by 17 U.S.C. Section 104.[35]

Published and unpublished works

For the most part the developers of ideas are concerned with their expression once they have entered a public arena of some kind. In order to protect a work which is published in the United States one need only affix a notice on all copies which provides:

Notice of copyright

1. The symbol a or the word "Copyright" or the abbreviation "Copr."
2. The year of first publication (can be omitted on pictorial, graphic or sculptural work).
3. The name or recognizable abbreviation of the name of the owner.   (17 U.S.C. Section 401).

No administrative proceeding is necessary to establish copyright as is the case with patent. The notice itself establishes the claim of right by warning the reader or user of the claim of ownership. Thus the statute requires that the notice "be affixed to the copies in such a manner and location as to give reasonable notice of the claim of copyright" (17 U.S.C. Section 401).

A further step is required in order to protect any work (published or unpublished) under the act. The act provides that one must register the work by depositing a copy of it with the copyright office prior to commencing a federal infringement action (17 U.S.C. Section 411). This is accomplished by applying for registration and depositing copies of the best edition of the work. The application and deposit must be in accord with the regulations of the copyright office. In general, however, approval and registry of the claim should be forthcoming, because the copyright office examines it only to see if the "material deposited constitutes copyrightable subject matter and that other legal and formal requirements have been met . . . "[36] By contrast, the issuance of a patent requires detailed investigation and approval by the patent office.

Registration—a precondition to remedies

The deposit of a computer program in the Copyright Office poses special problems. As with all such deposits, it becomes part of the public records of the Copyright Office and is available for public inspection.[37] Applicants

---

35. Prior to 1978 unpublished works were not subject to federal copyright, but were protected by common law copyright. Common law copyright was effectively abolished by the 1976 Copyright Act, although certain similar protection exists under state trade secret law now.

36. 17 U.S.C. Section 410.

37. 17 U.S.C. Section 701(d), 705(b) and 706(b).

may be justifiably concerned about the confidentiality of what may be a valuable business asset or competitive edge. Thus, the Copyright Office has recently allowed registration of computer programs in the following manner: first and last 25 pages of object code plus any 10 or more consecutive pages of unaltered source code; or first and last 10 pages of unaltered source code alone; or first and last 25 pages of source code with some portions deleted (but less than the material remaining).[38] A petition for "special relief" from the usual deposit requirement is necessary.[39]

Who may own copyrights?

In general, anyone may own a copyright to an expression. The basic rule is that "copyright in a work protected under this title vests initially in the author or authors of the work."[40] This usually means the actual creator or author. However "in the case of a work made for hire, the employer or other person for whom the work was prepared is considered the author"[41] for the purposes of copyright. If the employment relationship is one in which the employee's scope of activities specifically includes the obligation to create works of authorship, then the employer will own all the rights which comprise copyright, unless the employer and the employee have agreed otherwise in writing.[42] The better rule of law is that this applies only in those situations where the scope of employment rather specifically requires authorship and does not mean that employers are generally the owners of the employee's work.[43] This matter is covered in more detail in chapter 3, page 53.

The author, then, is the initial owner of a work and its copyright. That person or entity may transfer ownership of the copyright to another, who then owns the copyright.

Copyright of software

It is now firmly established that computer software may be copyrighted. Software in the form of source code which can be understood by humans directly is protected as a form of literature. It was not so easy for the courts to be sure that object code and other forms of software were protectable under copyright, because these are for practical purposes not directly understandable by humans. The source code of a program is a series of statements not unlike a recipe for a cake. When it is converted to object code, it is restated in pure binary numbers which are then usable by the machine. When these binary commands are recorded or fixed in a small chip (a "read only memory" or ROM) are they copyrightable?

---

38. Proposed rules appearing in 51 Fed. Register 34667, Sept. 30, 1986.
39. 37 C.F.R. 202.20(D) (1986).
40. 17 U.S.C. Section 201.
41. 17 U.S.C. Section 201(b).
42. 17 U.S.C. Section 201(b) and see Murray v. Gelderman, 566 F.2d 1307 (1978) and 11 A.L.R. Fed 457 (1972).
43. *Id.* at 1310.

The courts have now ruled that the content of ROM is copyrightable. The ROM need not be directly intelligible by a human. So long as the ROM ultimately communicates a message to a human it may be protectable by copyright. "Under the statute, copyright extends to works in any tangible means of expression *'from which they can be perceived,* reproduced, or otherwise communicated, either directly or indirectly or *with the aid of a machine or device.'* "[44] Thus the courts have held that many essential computer processes which express or carry commands are protectable, including ROMs and operations programs.

Following are additional observations which may help to indicate the boundaries of computer software and hardware copyright.

A utilitarian object is not itself copyrightable. Utilitarian objects are not protected by copyright law. This has long been the rule in the United States, and it is reflected in certain specific language in the 1976 Copyright Act. The 1976 Act grants protection to the artistic aspects of pictorial, graphic and sculptural works, but denies it insofar as "their mechanical or utilitarian aspects are concerned."[45] This limitation is further buttressed by the language of 17 U.S.C. Section 102 which denies copyright to processes, systems, and methods of operation, as mentioned earlier. However, recall that utilitarian objects are patentable.

The computer process must ultimately communicate—but with what or whom? The copyrightability of an operations program— one that communicates solely within the internal workings of a machine, directing its processes without any expression to a human being—is currently the subject of some controversy. Recent judicial decisions indicate that such programs, as well as object codes embedded in ROMs, are indeed copyrightable.[46]

Opponents of this theory argue that the intent of the copyright laws is to protect expressions that communicate to humans, and thus an object code or operations program should not be the subject of copyright.[47] How-

44. Apple Computer, Inc. v. Franklin Computer Corp., 714 F.2d 1240 at 1248 (3d Cir., 1983), cert. denied, 464 U.S. 1033 (1984).

45. Baker v. Selden, 101 U.S. 99 (1879), and 17 U.S.C. Section 101, definition of "Pictorial, graphic and sculptural works."

46. *See* M. Kramer Mfg. Co., Inc. v. Andrews, 783 F.2d 421, 435 (4th Cir. 1986); Apple Computer, Inc. v. Franklin Computer Corp., 714 F.2d 1240, 1247–48 (3d Cir. 1983), cert. denied, 464 U.S. 1033 (1984); and Apple Computer Inc. v. Formula Intern., Inc., 725 F.2d 521, 525 (9th Cir. 1984).

47. *See* Note, *The Semiconductor Chip Act: A New Weapon in the War Against Computer Software Piracy,* 1986 UTAH L. REV. 417, 433; Note, *Computer Copyright Law: An Emerging Form of Protection for Object Code Software After Apple v. Franklin,* 5 COMP. L.J. 233, 253 (1984). The author supports this view. For example, if instructions are built into a computer program that controls some part

ever, one case which held that an object code embedded in an ROM and an operations system are subject to copyright expressly rejected this theory, stating that the law requires only that the material communicate, not necessarily to humans.[48]

Video games provide a useful example of protected software. In *Atari v. North American Phillips Consumer Electric Corporation*, 672 F.2d 607 (Eighth Cir., 1982) the court granted substantial protection to the expressions contained in the Pac-Man Game while denying protection to the game itself. Because ideas themselves are not subject to copyright, the court stated, "it follows that copyright protection does not extend to games as such." The court then determined that it must "attempt to distill the protectable forms of expression in Pac-Man from the game itself."[49] The protectable matter involved was the particular expression of the video characters: the distinctive gobbler (Pac-Man) and the pursuing "ghost monsters." Such protections have included the imagery in a video game even when it is manipulated and changed by a player during the course of playing the game (*Williams Electronics, Inc. v. Artic Electronic International, Inc.*, 685 F.2d 870 [Third Cir., 1982]).

Chip protection. Recent federal legislation known as the Semiconductor Chip Protection Act (the "Act") has specifically extended protection to the semiconductor chip.[50] The Act protects (in intermediate or final form) "mask works," which are basically the patterns or blueprints for semiconductors, embedded in the circuitry of an actual semiconductor.[51] The original mask work is protected from copying for a period of ten years from either registration or first commercial exploitation, whichever occurs first.[52]

Registration of the mask work with the Register of Copyrights is optional, but carries the advantage of entitling the owner to statutory damages of up to $250,000 without having to prove actual damages in an action against an infringer.[53] Protection under the Act ends if a mask work is not registered within two years of its first commercial exploitation.[54] Notice of protection

---

of an automobile engine, these should not be viewed as subject to copyright. They are not part of any process that communicates to a human. Nor is it sufficient that the item concerned aid a communication process. Thus, neither a computerized ignition system, nor a light bulb in a movie projector should be subject to copyright.
48. Apple Computer, Inc. v. Franklin Computer Corp., 714 F.2d 1240, 1248 (3d Cir. 1983), cert. denied, 464 U.S. 1033 (1984).
49. 672 F.2d at 615.
50. 17 U.S.C. Sections 901 901–914.
51. 17 U.S.C. Section 901(a)(1) and (2).
52. 17 U.S.C. Section 901(a) and (b).
53. 17 U.S.C. Section 911(a).
54. 17 U.S.C. Section 908(a).

may be affixed to the mask work. Although notice is not a prerequisite to protection, it constitutes prima facie evidence of protection.[55]

The Act contains an exception to its prohibition against copying similar to the "fair use" doctrine under the Copyright Act.[56] Copying of a mask work is permitted for the purposes of "teaching, analyzing, or evaluating the concepts or techniques embodied in the mask work."[57] Moreover, one who gleans information in such a way may incorporate those ideas in his or her own mask work, so long as that work is "original."[58]

Because the Act does not exclude copyright or patent protection for semiconductor chips, double protection is possible for a program embodied in a chip. Double protection gives the owner the advantage of his choice of pursuing either actual or statutory protection under the Act for infringements occurring within ten years of initial registration plus the longer-term protection provided by the Copyright Act.[59]

Ownership rights

The owner of a copyright has the exclusive rights to reproduce the works, prepare derivative works, and distribute copies for a term equal to the life of the author plus 50 years. In addition, with respect to musical, artistic, and other such works, the owner has the exclusive right to display or perform the work.[60] Infringement occurs when there is copying or any other violation of these rights (17 U.S.C. Section 501).

Copying is obvious when a work is taken and reproduced on a copy machine or when there is direct and obvious plagiarism.[61] It is not necessary, however, that the copyright plaintiff have direct evidence in copying. In order to establish a prima facie case, the owner need demonstrate only that the defendant had access to the owner's work and that there is substantial similarity between that work and the allegedly infringing work.[62]

The principal defense in a copyright infringement case is the claim that the defendant's action constituted fair use of the copyrighted material. The fair use doctrine allows limited copying for such purposes as "criticism, comment, news reporting, teaching . . . , scholarship, or research" (17 U.S.C Section 107). In determining whether the use for these or other purposes is fair, courts will consider:

---

55. 17 U.S.C. Section 909(a).
56. See Section 2.17 below.
57. 17 U.S.C. Section 906(a)(1).
58. 17 U.S.C. Section 906(a)(2).
59. Works are protected for the lifetime of the author plus 50 years under the Copyright Act. See page 23.
60. 17 U.S.C. Sections 106 and 107. A different system exists as to sound recordings which are governed by compulsory licensing provisions under 17 U.S.C. Sections 114 and 115.
61. Nikanov v. Simon Schuster, Inc., 246 F.2d 501 (2d Cir., 1957).
62. Walker v. University Books, Inc., 602 F.2d 859, 864 (9th Cir., 1979).

1. The purpose and character of the use
2. Whether it is for profit
3. The nature of the work copied
4. The amount or proportion of the work used
5. The effect of the use on the potential market or value of the work[63]

A departure from fair use is often detected where the user (copier) derives a substantial monetary or economic benefit from the material copied. For example, when the publisher of a gardening book copied a listing of plant and seed suppliers, the court held that this was not fair use, in part, because the copying allowed the producers of this second book "to meet an important deadline."[64]

In 1961 the Registrar of Copyright described examples which would likely be considered fair use:

> ... quotation of excerpts in a review or criticism for purposes of illustration or comment; quotation of short passages in a scholarly or technical work, for illustration or clarification of the author's observations; use in a parody of some of the content of the work parodied; summary of an address or article, with brief quotations, in a news report; reproduction by a library of a portion of a work to replace part of a damaged copy; reproduction by a teacher or a student of a small part of a work to illustrate a lesson; reproduction of a work in legislative or judicial proceedings or reports; incidental and fortuitous reproduction, in a newsreel or broadcast, of a work located in the scene of an event being reported.[65]

The fair use doctrine was given express statutory recognition for the first time in 17 U.S.C. Section 107 enacted in 1976. The House Report accompanying the legislation specifically cited the same examples quoted above, giving them an authoritative basis for gauging what is fair.

In addition, the law provides for a specific form of fair use which is important to computer producers, developers, and users. The owner of a copy of a computer program is permitted to make either a copy or adaptation of the program if: the copy is necessary to make the program compatible with or usable by a particular machine; or the copy is kept for archival or backup purposes.[66] Although this specific section refers only to "owners" as having this privilege, it is the author's opinion that a "licensee" or

---

63. 17 U.S.C. Section 107.

64. Schroeder v. William Morrow and Company, 566 F.2d 3, 6 (7th Cir., 1977).

65. As noted in the text, the examples of the Registrar of Copyright have been authoritatively quoted in the HOUSE REPORT ON THE COPYRIGHT ACT, HR 94-1476 (1976); 1976 U.S. CODE CONG. & AD. NEWS 5659, 5678–79.

66. 17 U.S.C. Section 117 and Micro-Sparc, Inc. v. Amtype Corp., 592 F. Supp. 33 (D. Mass. 1984) (placing on disks programs appearing in computer magazine and selling the disks did not constitute copying for archival purposes).

privileged user of a program should be likewise free from liability for infringement under the same circumstances.[67]

Since copyright is achieved when the work exists in a tangible form and proper notice in all published versions is given, it presents the advantages of speed, simplicity, and absence of bureaucratic difficulties. The legal remedies require the additional step of registration, but this, too, is simple and direct. In the highly competitive environment of high tech development, where speed to the market is prized, copyright is an excellent means of protection.

One owns a copyrighted work as soon as it is fixed in a tangible means of expression. If the expression can ultimately be understood by a human, with or without the aid of a machine, it is protectable. To retain copyright of a published work, it is necessary to affix the required notice of copyright, name, and date to each copy. The term of a copyright is the life of the author plus fifty years. The owner of a copyright generally has the exclusive right to reproduce the work, prepare derivative works, and distribute copies. Unlike an owner of a patent, a copyright holder does not have an exclusive right to use the work unless the copyrighted work has been distributed under a restrictive license provision prior to the first sale.[68] It is not necessary to have a copyright approval before it exists as in the case of patent. Registration, however, is a precondition to enforcement of the copyright.

Trade secrets

Patent law and copyright law each create a legal shield which accompanies the product and protects the creator's legal property rights. Trade secret law differs in that it relies primarily (and nearly exclusively) on the continuous efforts of the developer to protect himself or herself. Trade secret protection is essentially self-help. "A valuable development may be protected by trade secret law, but the necessary and constant condition is

---

67. The position stated in the text relies on 17 U.S.C. Section 107 together with 17 U.S.C. Section 117.

68. A detailed discussion on the use of licenses to protect intellectual property is beyond the scope of this book. I wish to note briefly, however, that licenses and the doctrine of first sale developed in cases dealing with motion picture copyrights are an extremely powerful means of protecting intellectual property in the computer area. *See* United Artists Television, Inc. v. Fortnightly Corp., 377 F.2d 872 (2d Cir., 1967). I wish especially to thank Mr. Gervaise Davis III Esquire, of Monterey, California, for his suggestions regarding this most important doctrine. See pages 31–32.

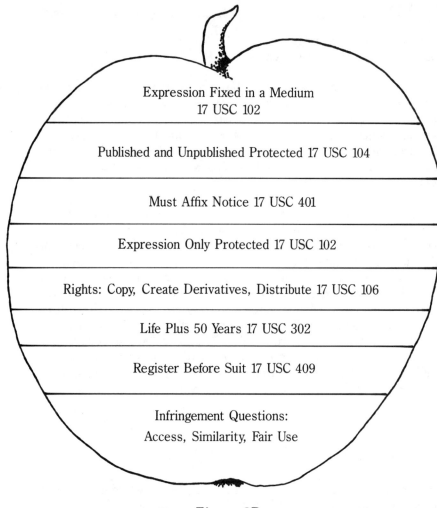

Figure 2B
COPYRIGHT PROTECTION

continued vigilance; even *accidental* disclosures may destroy trade secrets."[69]

Trade secret qualifications   In order to qualify as a trade secret a piece of information must be shown to be:

1. Economically valuable

---

69. Task Force on Legal Aspects of Computer Based Technology, *Protection of Computer Idea Work Today and Tomorrow*, IEEE SOFTWARE, April 1984, at 76. *See also* Section 3.12 infra.

2. Not generally known
3. Kept as a secret

These general elements appear in the definition of trade secret provided in the Restatement (First) of Torts and in the Uniform Trade Secret Act.[70] It is important to emphasize that trade secret law is subject to variation and redefinition on a state-by-state basis, although the basic principles and definitions remain rather stable.

It probably goes without saying that whether something is a trade secret depends upon the circumstances. Despite the fluidity of the concept, the following criteria are very helpful in making the judgment of whether a given process or methodology is a trade secret:

  . . . the extent to which the alleged trade secrets are ahead of industry
      awareness or replication, . . .

  . . . the extent to which the information is known outside the origi-
      nator's business;

  . . . the affirmative steps taken by the originator to guard against
      disclosure of the information, . . .

  . . . the value of the information to the originator and to his compet-
      itors;

  . . . the amount of money or effort expended by the originator in de-
      veloping the information; and

  . . . the ease or difficulty with which the information can be acquired
      or duplicated by others . . . [71]

Developers of high tech items

There are a number of constraints operating in the development process that make reliance on secrecy unavoidable. First of all, we have seen that ideas and general approaches or methods are neither patentable nor copyrightable. Secondly, even if general processes (e.g., algorithms) were to achieve more legal protection, the speed of development and changes in markets would cause developers to rely on "hush-hush" procedures rather than legal property rights in many instances.

The software developer or other high tech worker will predictably rely on secrecy in instances such as:

1. Initial *conception* of an approach to a problem. For example, one
   might develop a basic approach to solving hearing or vision defects.

---

70. Section 757 of the Restatement (First) of Torts and The Uniform Trade Secrets Act are set forth in the Appendix.

71. Task Force on Legal Aspects of Computer Based Technology, *Protection of Computer Idea Work Today and Tomorrow*, IEEE SOFTWARE, April 1984, at 76.

2. Translation of the concept to an *initial design*. Again, the basic system of an improved hearing aid would be roughed out.
3. *Essential components* need to be designed. The basic system for the hearing aid might be shown to selective co-workers so that specific elements can be designed.
4. An *algorithm* may be involved in the design. The hearing aid might use a particular algorithm in its design. If closely enough tied to the hardware, the use of the algorithm may be protectable by patent (see pages 12–14).
5. Specific *suppliers* or subcontractors may be necessary. The developer may wish to keep the identity of these suppliers secret.
6. *Marketing* or distribution channels may be selected and contacted. Lists of specific dealers for the hearing aid might be established.

Each of these items will be valuable in the development of the product and related business. The design and its components might in some instances be protected by copyright or patent, but until they are, the developer will want to control them and protect their confidential nature. The supplier and marketing information can generally only be protected by trade secret methods.

Practical problems   The holder of trade secrets faces difficult choices. The secret is valuable. However, to realize its value there must be cooperation with others and access to a market. More harm than good can be done by heavy-handed efforts to preserve secrecy. Employees and colleagues will not respond favorably to a "police state" working environment, and customers may be discouraged by burdensome contracts or licensing agreements. The developer must therefore choose wisely from the techniques available to protect secrets.

1. In-house protection

Confidentiality agreements with employees and co-workers. These are a tried and effective way of controlling the access to information. For restrictions on these, see pages 54–62.

Control of access to information by department, "need to know" limits, and similar restrictions.

Specific identification of sensitive items so in-house workers and colleagues know what must be protected. This is very important. Certainly the company should distinguish clearly between the location of the coffee machine and the specifications of a critical part of a process.

Routine and special contacts with employees working on projects. These contacts allow the company to learn what is new and important in the employee's work and give the employer an opportunity to inform the employee what should be kept strictly confidential.

Restrictions regarding outside contacts. Great caution should be exercised by employers in using such restrictions. Unfortunately this is often not the case. It is fair to restrict the employee regarding the content of certain conversations with others and to caution regarding certain settings and contacts that might be risky. However, this is a mobile society and heavy restriction of this type is seen as an invasion of privacy and is resented.

Debriefing employees. Debriefing is a military term. It means to instruct and interrogate regarding secret data. Thoughtful (and pointed) conversations with an employee before or after a trip or a conference or at other critical times may be useful. It is my view that a rigid or pushy process of this kind is totally inappropriate and self-defeating. Abuse in this area can lead to the feeling that the company is a "police state."

Exit interviews. When an employee leaves employment, he or she ought to be interviewed. The employee should be reminded of his or her obligations. To be effective the interview should note specifics of what should be kept confidential. See pages 58–67.

2. *Protection in the marketplace.*

Trade secrets can be disclosed to others outside a business without losing their protection *if* precautions are taken. These include notice, nondisclosure agreements, licenses, and contract provisions. In some instances, as during negotiations for sale of a business or establishing a joint venture, notice of the secret nature may be enough. Often, however, a more formal recognition such as a confidentiality agreement is called for.

When a product, for example, a computer program, is distributed to customers or the public, it is important to consider the restriction of the use of information which might be embodied in the distribution process. For example, the company may consider:

Sale or lease with restriction on dissemination. The contract itself may be drafted so that the buyer is obligated not to disclose certain items.

Licensing rather than sale. A stronger means of protection is generally available by a grant of use without transfer of any form of ownership or property. Thus, a developer may wish to license only certain specified uses of a particular process. This licensing approach may be appropriate even if the material involved is copyrighted. (See pages 30–31 regarding licensing.)

These methods of protection are sketched out here to demonstrate how trade secrets may be protected. It is, however, well beyond the scope of this book to describe specifically how these techniques and others should be employed.

Remedies for misappropriation of trade secrets

Trade secrets enjoy the protection of the full panoply of legal remedies. In appropriate cases, injunctions will be granted by courts to protect trade secrets. Also, damages to compensate for the loss are available in most cases.[72]

Other aspects of intellectual property law

Confidentiality

There are other ways in which the law protects idea work. Confidential information which has not coalesced into a trade secret may be protectable. Examples of this kind of information might include suggestions, options, or questions of timing discussed at a general planning meeting of a company.

Trademarks, business names, and such marketing information as customer lists are subject to protection. Trademarks can be protected under federal and state law. Customer lists are actually a form of trade secret, a form which probably has been more frequently litigated than any other. Such lists when kept secret are definitely protectable.[73]

Laws of confidentiality may be useful when ideas or idea products are valuable, but do not lend themselves readily to protection by the patent, copyright, or trade secret. For instance, in the United States and elsewhere certain types of television programs have great audience appeal. The idea for a timely or "catchy" new program is valuable. A number of years ago, a man named Faris conceived of an idea for an interesting sports quiz show. He disclosed his idea to Enberg, an employee of a television station, in hopes of getting the station to enter into a production contract with him. Instead the station produced a variation of the show without including Faris![74] The *Faris* case presents a situation that might be called a "pure

---

72. Roger Milgrim, *Trade Secrets*, 12 BUSINESS ORGANIZATIONS, Section 7.08 (1983).

73. A customer list can be protected by copyright, but this is primarily of value to one who wishes to publish and profit from dissemination of the list itself, as copyright law prohibits copying but does not prohibit use of the list itself.

74. Faris v. Enberg, 97 Cal. App. 3d 309, 158 Cal. Rptr. 704 (1979). The comments in this section were originally delivered as a talk to the Modern Law Research Center of Sapporo Gakuin University Law School, in Sapporo, Japan in the summer of 1985. I wish to thank the center's director, Professor Kazuaki Uda, and his colleagues for that opportunity. The substance of these remarks was published first in the 1985 SAPPORO GAKUIN UNIVERSITY MODERN LAW RESEARCH CENTER: ANNUAL REPORT, 1985, 8–14.

idea" case. His idea was a general one. Since it was an idea only and was not reduced to the form of an invention or an expression, it could not qualify for patent or copyright protection. Nevertheless, the court recognized that such an idea might qualify for some kind of legal protection. The court did not acknowledge any kind of a "property right" in the idea, but it did examine the course of conduct between the idea man, Faris, and the TV studio. If the idea for the sports show had been given by Faris to Enberg in confidence, then Enberg and the station might be liable to Faris if they took and exploited the value of the idea.[75] Faris ultimately lost his case, because he failed to demonstrate that he had made it clear that he would only disclose his ideas if that disclosure were treated as confidential.

The author or developer will usually want to disclose ideas in order to make use of them. The law of confidentiality may protect ideas that are disclosed in a controlled and limited fashion. The risks involved in unguarded disclosures are loss of control and loss of profit. The California Supreme Court stated the matter bluntly in *Desny v. Wilder*: "the idea man who blurts out his idea without having first made his bargain has no one but himself to blame for the loss of his bargaining power."[76]

As the quotation from the *Desny* case indicates, contract is the primary method that business people and lawyers use to limit the scope of their disclosures. A bargain is struck at various phases in the development of new processes. These agreements usually take the following general forms:

Non-disclosure agreements at the outset of negotiations—"I will disclose, if you agree to keep secret and not use without approval."

Development contracts—these contracts provide for the production of certain processes to certain specifications and require the producer to preserve as confidential those processes and other items which are employed.

Licensing agreements—"We will allow you to use this process in the following ways." (See pages 30–31.)

While it is essential to make confidentiality arrangements at the outset, before one discloses, there is concomitant risk—people may be discouraged from dealing with you if you begin your discussions by brandishing a host of legal obligations! There are the practical problems of judgment and tact. How can one approach another in hopes of interesting him or her, yet take some steps to protect the idea involved? If it is judged that the other party is ready or willing to make a formal commitment to confidentiality, then that can be done. If that is not the case, for example, during one's very first contact, then a more informal means of giving notice may be

75. 97 Cal. App. 3d 309, 323.
76. 46 Cal. 2d 715, 739, 299 P.2d 257 (1956).

employed. Basically, if an innovator lets the other party know that what he is about to reveal is confidential *before* he discloses it, then there is a very good argument that the other party will be obliged to preserve the confidence as long as the idea is novel and the recipient has been given the opportunity to refuse to hear it. That approach does give substantial protection to the innovator, but at the same time obliges him to act with some care. He must give the other side a chance to say: "We do not want to hear that idea."[77] One way that this can be done is to place a phone call to the party in advance of the initial meeting and state that you wish to discuss confidential ideas with the person at your scheduled meeting, and that it is necessary to treat the matters as confidential. This conversation might then be confirmed in a confirming letter sent so as to be received in advance of the conference.

It is wise to consider consulting with a lawyer before disclosing really valuable ideas to others. It is a situation where an ounce of prevention is worth more than a pound of cure.

Licensing   A license is simply a grant of permission allowing someone to do something. Licensing is one of the most significant and important areas of the law of intellectual property, because people who have developed idea products wish to put them into the hands of others who can produce or market them. Most often a license is embodied in a contract. That is, the person who wishes to grant permission to another will make an agreement with the second person, and the license will be spelled out and made part of a binding contract. It is important to recognize, however, that it is not necessary that a license be founded upon a bargained agreement or contract. For example, a software developer may discover that someone plans to use his software in an unauthorized demonstration or workshop. For a variety of reasons, it may be advantageous to avoid bringing pressure on this user—it may be worthwhile to develop friendly relations with that person as a prospective consumer, for example. One way to preserve one's rights while avoiding any pressuring communications is to give notice of one's rights while granting a strictly limited (and non-contractual) use license for the specific event in question.[78]

Detailed coverage of licensing is beyond the scope of this book. A word of caution may be helpful to the developer concerning licensing. It is extremely important to plan and draft licenses with care. A lot of trouble and

---

77. *See* Tel Account Engineers, Inc. v. Pacific Telephone and Telegraph Company, 168 Cal. App. 3d 455, 214 Cal. Rptr. 276 (1985).

78. The substance of the observations in this paragraph originally appeared in a book review I prepared for the Santa Clara University Law School, COMPUTER AND HIGH TECHNOLOGY LAW REVIEW, Volume III, Number 2, (1987), page 405.

misunderstanding may be avoided if clarity is achieved in a license. Again, wisdom counsels one to seek the help of a skilled lawyer in this area.

Crimes

For the most part we are concerned with civil remedies to protect intellectual property. However, it should be noted that all the major forms of intellectual property are covered by criminal laws as well. In certain instances violation of proprietary rights may be prosecuted as a crime.

Under the patent laws, willfully false statements on patent documents;[79] falsely holding oneself out to be recognized to practice before the Patent and Trademark Office;[80] willful publication of material ordered secret;[81] and falsely marking an article as patented[82] are all subject to criminal penalties. The Copyright Act makes criminal the following acts: infringement for purposes of commercial or financial gain; fraudulent copyright notices or removal thereof; and the making of a false statement in an application for copyright registration.[83] Violation of a trade secret right may be a criminal offense under state law.[84] In addition, there may be liability under federal law for interstate transportation of stolen goods under 18 U.S.C. Section 2314 or for mail fraud under 18 U.S.C. Section 1314.

Reverse engineering

Reverse engineering is simply the process of taking something apart to see how it works.[85] Once this is done it may be possible to figure out how to build a precisely similar item just from the information gained by taking it apart. If the item disassembled contains no patented, copyrighted, or licensed material, or material otherwise protected by trade secret, then it appears that remanufacture of new items based on the information learned is perfectly legal. The logic supporting this conclusion is straightforward: if no patent, no copyright, and no trade secret is taken, there is, in effect, no "property" which is misappropriated in the remanufacture.

The Supreme Court has stated:

> The law also protects the holder of a trade secret against disclosure or use when the knowledge is gained, not by the owner's volition, but by some "improper means," Restatement of Torts, Section 757(a), which may include theft, wiretapping, or even aerial reconnaissance. A trade secret law, however, does not offer protection against discovery by fair and honest means, such as by independent invention, accidental disclosure, or by so-called reverse engineering, that is by starting with the known product and working

---

79. 35 U.S.C. Section 25(b) and 18 U.S.C. Section 1001.
80. 35 U.S.C. Section 33.
81. 35 U.S.C. Sections 182 and 186.
82. 35 U.S.C. Section 292.
83. 17 U.S.C. Section 506.
84. *See* Annot., 84 A.L.R. 3d 967 (1978).
85. Kewanee Oil Co. v. Bicron Corp., 416 U.S. 470, 476 (1974).

backward to divine the process which aided in its development or manufacture.[86]

It should be noted that reverse engineering is unobjectionable only in its "pure" form. That is, if the process is aided by the use of trade secret material, then there may be liability for the use of that material.

Reverse engineering also becomes relevant in determining whether a process is secret or not. "Reverse engineering time is certainly a factor in determining whether information is readily ascertainable."[87] Thus, if a product is produced or reproduced far more swiftly than either direct engineering or reverse engineering would permit, there may be an inference that secret information was used.

State, federal, and international law

Copyright and patent law are purely matters of federal statutory law. Thus, where these two bodies of law come directly into play they govern to the exclusion of state law. State law may in some instances be preempted. As a general proposition, however, the broad body of state trade secret law is not preempted by federal law.[88] Since state law governs trade secrets, there may be variation from state to state.

The fields of patent, copyright, and trade secret law have a firm and long-established basis in United States constitutional law and state law. Nevertheless, since these areas of law have an impact on free circulation of ideas, there is the distinct possibility that certain intellectual property claims will reach too far and conflict with policies that favor free circulation of ideas.

An example of the impact of the United States Constitution on the law of intellectual property law is *Sony Corporation v. Universal City Studios*, 464 U.S. 417, 104 S. Ct. 774 (1984). In the *Sony* case, Universal Studios and Walt Disney Productions contended that the primary use of Sony's Betamax video tape recorders was to record and reproduce copyrighted television programming. The studios contended that since Sony knew that homeowners would use the recorders for this purpose, it should be held accountable for copyright violations. The Ninth Circuit Court of Appeals agreed with the studios' contentions and provided for relief against Sony. The Supreme Court reversed, holding that no violation of the copyright laws had been shown. The court ruled that the record showed that the Betamax machine could be used for substantial purposes which do not infringe copyright. In reaching this conclusion the court emphasized that the monopoly conferred by copyright laws "must ultimately serve the cause

---

86. 416 U.S. at 475–476.
87. Electrocraft Corp. v. Controlled Motion, 332 N.W.2d 890, 899 (Minn. 1983).
88. 17 U.S.C. Section 301 and Kewanee Oil Co. v. Bicron Corp., 416 U.S. 470 (1974).

of promoting broad public availability of literature, music and the other arts."[89]

There is an international dimension which is becoming more important. Protection of all forms of intellectual property which enter into foreign commerce or which may be duplicated elsewhere will be protected outside of the United States only to the extent that international treaties, doctrines of reciprocity, or local law give recognition and protection.

The major forms of intellectual property offer different advantages and disadvantages. Patents tend to be difficult to obtain but sturdy in the protection offered, however, they are unlikely to be granted for software. Copyright is easy to establish for virtually any form of fixed expression. It is now a proven mechanism for protecting many aspects of computer development. Trade secret protection is the only one which offers some protection for ideas per se, but it is awkward because of its dependence on secrecy.

The common substance of all these forms of protection is intellectual work. The developers—employer and employee—will often struggle over the ownership of the work product. We now turn full attention to that contest.

Concluding observations

---

89. 464 U.S. 417, 432, 104 S.Ct. 774, 783.

CHAPTER 3

The Employment Relationship

Importance of the relationship

The nature of the employment relationship and the specific conditions upon which employment is undertaken are critical in determining who owns idea work products. Indeed, these conditions will often determine who has the right to idea work products.[1]

The employment relationship that we will examine is made up of several components:

1. The employment contract (express or implied)
2. Legal rules or policies which exist independent of the bargaining process
3. Employment rules such as employee manuals
4. Actual practices within the specific employment environment
5. Legitimate expectations of the parties

These factors fit together to form an entire fabric that will determine individual and company rights in each specific context. The results will differ from case to case since the weight of these factors changes from case to case. Nevertheless, basic principles and guidelines exist.

The employment contract

The employment relationship in the United States is usually viewed as being a contract. This means that either party is theoretically free to bargain for any employment conditions subject to certain limitations. Free-

---

1. I have referred to "intellectual work products" (or "idea work products") because not all claims to important ideas and uses amount to "intellectual property," that is, protected by law. Please refer to Chapters 1 and 2, especially pages 3–4 and 7–8.

dom of contract in the field of employment is now governed by a variety of laws and policies such as antidiscrimination laws, antitrust policies, and rules against illegal contracts. The basic point is, however, that, with exceptions, the employment relationship is one created and governed by contract whether the contract be expressed or implied. Because of the contractual nature of employment, the terms of the employment contract will be critical in any determination of employer and employee claims to idea work product. This point is emphasized in the following guideline.

GUIDELINE ONE

Contract Terms
It is critical that the employer and the employee take full account of express and implied terms of the contract. This is true in bargaining for employment and in carrying out the relationship.

Implied terms

While it is true that the employment relationship is basically contractual, it is equally true that there are large measures of public policy that condition that contract. In order to understand this, we should take a brief look at the way United States law has evolved. The theory that one should be free to make his or her contracts regarding employment is attractive. One should enjoy the freedom to engage or disengage from a job. The spirit of this freedom was captured by John Campbell in 1872 when he argued to the United States Supreme Court in the *Slaughter-House* cases:

> The obligation to labor being imperious, confers a right to labor, which right is property; and it can not be withdrawn or destroyed by arbitrary legislation without the violation of natural right.[2]

This approach gave rise to a theory of law which held that if the employee is free to quit his or her job, the employer must be equally free to terminate the employment.[3] As one court has stated, "in the absence of a statute or an agreement an employer may discharge his employee for cause or without cause . . . " unless the contract specifies otherwise.[4]

The realities of modern employment are far different than the theory of contract suggests, however. The employer is usually quite able to replace

---

2. 21 L.Ed. 395, 397 (1872).

3. Peter Linzer, *The Decline of Assent: At-Will Employment as a Case Study of the Breakdown of Private Law Theory*, 20 Ga. L. Rev. 323, 336 (1986); Note, *Employee Handbooks and Employment-at-Will Contracts*, 1985 Duke L.J. 196, 197 (1985); *see also* Ellen Russ Pierce, Richard A. Mann, and Barry S. Roberts, *Employee Termination At Will; A Principled Approach*, 28 Vill. L. Rev. 1, 6 (1982).

4. Conrad v. Delta Airlines, Inc., 494 F.2d 914, 916 (7th Cir., 1974).

the terminated employee, while that person is usually far less able to find a suitable replacement job or perhaps any job at all. The terminated employee is often in a far more vulnerable economic position as well, with living expenses to meet and little or no income to meet them. Nor is the employee often in a position to demand certain favorable contractual provisions at the time of initial employment. Such doctrines as the employer's right to terminate employment at will have allowed the employer to rule "the workplace with an ironhand."[5]

All of this has caused some courts to recognize that freedom of contract needs to be counterbalanced by legal doctrines that protect the employee. Indeed, many courts have recognized that termination of employment may be conditioned by an employer's obligation to act in good faith or acknowledge an implied term of the contract not to terminate without cause.[6] The evolution of contract law has created implied terms of contract and certain other restrictions on the employment relation.[7] These include:

The obligation of good faith. Courts have often insisted that the parties of a contract owe each other good faith in the performance of the contract. "In every contract there is an implied covenant of good faith and fair dealing that neither party will do anything which injures the right of the other to receive the benefits of the agreement."[8] In the employment context, this general principle obliges both employer and employee to act together to accomplish their common goal. The employee is obliged not to interfere with the employer's projects, but rather to carry out his or her duties in good faith. The employer is obliged to treat the employee fairly in the context of the employment.

---

5. Monge v. Beebe Rubber Co., 114 N.H. 130, 316 A.2d 549 (1974).

6. Some states having such rulings are: California, Koehrer v. Superior Court, 181 Cal. App. 3d 1155, 226 Cal. Rptr. 820 (1986); Pugh v. See's Candies, Inc., 116 Cal. App. 3d 311 and 171 Cal. Reptr. 917 (1981); New Hampshire, Monge v. Beebe Rubber Co., 114 N.H. 130, 316 A.2d 549 (1974); Pennsylvania, McNulty v. Borden, Inc., 474 F. Supp. 1111 (E.D.Pa., 1979); Magnan v. Anaconda Industries, Inc., 429 A.2d 492 (Conn. 1980), Wagenseller v. Scottsdale Memorial Hosp., 710 P.2d 1025 (Ariz. 1985); Crinshaw v. Bozeman Deaconess Hosp., 693 P.2d 487 (Mont. 1984); Massachusetts, Siles v. Travenol Laboratories, 13 Mass. Ap. Ct. 354, 433 N.E.2d 103 (1982), appeal denied, 440 N.E.2d 1176 (1982).

7. Statements contained in a policy manual may also create enforceable rights. Woolley v. Hofmann-La Roche, Inc., 99 N.J. 284, 491 A.2d 1257 (1985); Kaiser v. Dixon, 127 Ill. App. 3d 251, 468 N.E.2d 822, 831 (1984) (employee entitled to benefit of termination notice and hearing described in employee policy manual); Note, *Employment Manual Ruled Implied Consent*, 8 AM. J. TRIAL ADV. 329 (1985).

8. Brown v. Superior Court, 34 Cal.2d 559, 212 P.2d 878 (1949) and Seaman's Direct Buying Serv., Inc. v. Standard Oil Co., 36 Cal.3d 752, 748, 206 Cal. Rptr. 354, 686 P.2d 1158 (1984). *See also* American Law Institute, Restatement (Second) of Contracts, Section 205, and Steven J. Burton, *Breach of Contract and the Common Law Duty to Perform in Good Faith*, 94 HARV. L. REV. 369 (1980–1981).

Duties of loyalty.   Not all employees will bear the same degree of obligation of performance to the employer. Some people are hired to carry out routine tasks while others are asked to exercise judgment, keep confidences, or carry through in a position of trust. As to employees in those positions, there may be a higher duty of loyalty or service. An employee in such a position is generally obliged to be far more careful "not to put himself in a position antagonistic" to that of his employer.[9] If one occupies a specific position of trust, one may be viewed as a fiduciary or trustee and will be obliged to exercise the highest good faith and loyalty in carrying out one's duties.[10]

Courts have had occasion to consider the duty of loyalty owed by corporate officers. It has often been stated that officers have a duty to preserve "corporate opportunities" for the benefit of the employer corporation.

> Briefly summarized, the law is that if a business opportunity is presented to a corporate executive, the officer can not seize the opportunity for himself if: (a) the corporation is financially able to undertake it; (b) it is within the corporation's line of business; (c) the corporation is interested in the opportunity.[11]

It is likely that such principles will be applied not only to officers, but to "key managerial personnel" and other pivotal persons whether labeled consultants or employees.[12]

GUIDELINE TWO

Good Faith

It is essential that the employer and employee treat each other with good faith as to their obligations and matters of common interest related to the employment.

Unconscionable contracts

The employment contract, like any other, is binding. The fact that it may be conditioned by implied terms as indicated in the previous section does not allow either party to ignore the express provisions.

> One who enters a contract is on notice of the provisions of the contract. If he assents voluntarily to those provisions after notice, he should be pre-

---

9. Science Accessories Corp. v. Summagraphics Corp., 425 A.2d 957 (Del. 1980).

10. Rader v. Thrasher, 59 Cal. 2d 244, 249, 368 P.2d 360 (1962) and Rieger v. Rich, 163 Cal. App. 2d 651, 665, 329 P.2d 770 (1958).

11. Science Accessories Corp. v. Summagraphics Corp., 425 A.2d 957, 963 (Del. 1980). *See also* Weismann v. Snyder, 338 Mass. 502, 156 N.E.2d 21 (1959), and Annot., 17 A.L.R.4th 479 (1982).

12. 425 A.2d 957, 962 (Del. 1980).

sumed, in the absence of ambiguity, to have understood and agreed to comply with the provisions as written.[13]

Despite this general rule, there are certain critical exceptions, among which is the doctrine of unconscionability.[14]

Courts will often refuse to enforce contracts or terms of contracts which are notably unfair. This is a growing development in contract law. "If a contract or a term thereof is unconscionable at the time the contract is made a court may refuse to enforce the contract, or may enforce the remainder of the contract without the unconscionable term, or may so limit the application of any unconscionable term as to avoid any unconscionable result."[15]

In 1889 the United States Supreme Court applied the principle to strike down a contract which would have allowed a seller to receive forty times the market value of his product, the agreement being "a grossly unconscionable bargain."[16] This principle has long played an important role in commercial transactions and is embodied in U.C.C. Section 2-302. In 1979, California enacted a civil code section which makes the principle specifically applicable to all contracts.[17]

The principle will surely play an especially prominent role in employer/employee relations. Today one's job is often the most important and sometimes most fragile of possessions. A law review article written twenty years ago by Matthew O. Tobriner and Joseph R. Grodin warned that in many circumstances contracts are so one-sided that "rigid reliance upon their terms as defining legal obligations between the parties may, in effect, produce new forms of subservience under the guise of contract."[18]

The critical inquiry is "what is unconscionable?" The basic approach is to detect what may objectively be described as unfair. Conditions and factors which may make the bargain unconscionable include:

Inadequate compensation. "Inadequacy of consideration does not of itself invalidate a bargain, but gross disparity in the values exchanged may be an important factor in a determination that a contract is unconscionable and may be sufficient ground, without more, for denying specific performance."[19]

---

13. Wallace v. Chafee, 451 F.2d 1374, 1377 (9th Cir., 1971), cert. denied, 409 U.S. 933 (1973).

14. *See also* pages 42–48 and 54–67.

15. Restatement (Second) of Contracts, Section 208.

16. Hume v. United States, 132 U.S. 406, 410 (1889).

17. CAL. CIV. CODE Section 1670.5.

18. Matthew O. Tobriner and Joseph R. Grodin, *The Individual and the Public Service Enterprise in the New Industrial State*, 55 CAL. L. REV. 1247, 1252 (1967).

19. Restatement (Second) of Contracts, Section 208, Comment C.

Disparity of bargaining power. If one party has very little choice in the matter because of economic or social circumstances, the agreement may be viewed as unconscionable.[20] In one Illinois case, an overly restrictive employee agreement was declared unconscionable when the employee was presented with the agreement after he had sold his home in another state and moved to Illinois, where he was told the agreement was a non-negotiable condition of employment.[21]

Failure to observe reasonable standards of fair dealing. There is a general standard of good faith in commercial dealings which allows a court to refer to standards of fair dealing that grow up within a trade.[22] This type of general standard may allow the employee who is party to a contract to bring forth proof of the actual practices of an industry, for example, employment or subcontracting practices in the software industry, to test the fairness of his or her argument.

Too hard a bargain. One of the critical aspects of a contract is the remedy to be applied if the contract is adhered to. Generally courts will offer only damages as a remedy, but if damages are not adequate to protect the disappointed party, then specific performance of the contract may be ordered. (Please see pages 67–69 on remedies.) While hard bargaining is generally permissible under the law, a court may refuse to enforce a provision that places one party in a very tight economic bind. A court may conclude that "the sum total of (a contract's) provisions drives too hard a bargain for a court of conscience to assist."[23]

Adhesion contracts. Often the available alternatives to one party are so substantially similar that he or she is offered little, if any, choice. Under these circumstances, the one party may be given a "take it or leave it" choice. Thus, an individual seeking a job may be faced with a series of employers all of which demand disclosure of all the individual's work product and assignment of all claims to such products. Within each company each employee may be required to sign substantially similar agreements. Such a contract may be an "adhesion contract," one "which, imposed and drafted by the party of superior bargaining strength, relegates to the subscribing party only the opportunity to adhere to the contract or reject

20. Henningsen v. Bloomfield Motors, Inc., 32 .J. 358, 161 A.2d 69, 87 (1960) and Hillman, *Debunking Some Myths About Unconscionability*, 67 Cornell L. Rev. 1, 30–31 (1982).

21. Disher v. Fulgoni, 124 Ill. App. 3d 257, 464 N.E.2d 639, 644 (1984).

22. U.C.C. 2–103. *See, e.g.*, Ashland Oil, Inc. v. Donohue, 223 S.E.2d 433 (1976).

23. Campbell Soup Co. v. Wentz, 172 F.2d 80 (3rd Cir., 1948) and *see* C & J Fertilizer, Inc. v. Allied Mutual Ins. Co., 227 N.W. 2d 169 (Iowa 1975).

it."[24] Adhesion contracts may be refused enforcement if their provisions do not fall within the reasonable expectations of the weaker party.

In *Graham v. Scissor-Tail, Inc.*,[25] a well-known San Francisco concert promoter, Bill Graham, entered into a standard contract with a musical group, Scissor-Tail. Even though Graham himself was experienced and commanded considerable bargaining strength, the court agreed that he had been "reduced to the humble role of 'adherent' to an all or nothing contract" by the dominant role of the American Federation of Musicians. This triggered an inquiry into whether a term of the contract concerning arbitration either failed to meet Graham's reasonable expectation or was unconscionable. While that provision was found to be unconscionable, the rest of the contract was allowed to stand even through it was "adhesive."[26] A contract may be adhesive, without necessarily being unconscionable.

In *Cubic Corporation v. Marty*, an employee of a corporation conceived and developed a new means of training pilots. While the idea was originally conceived by Marty independent of his employment, it was perfected with substantial assistance of the employer. Part of Marty's contract required him:

> To promptly disclose to Company all ideas, processes, inventions, improvements, developments and discoveries coming within the scope of Company's business or related to Company's products or to any research, design experimental or production work carried on by Company, or to any problems specifically assigned to Employee, conceived alone or with others during this employment, and whether or not conceived during regular working hours.[27]

The court found that the contract provision was part of an "adhesion contract." "Cubic drafted the contract, it gave its employees no opportunity to negotiate the terms, but rather offered it on a take-it-or-leave-it basis as a condition of employment at Cubic."[28] The court ruled, however, that the contract was valid as applied to Marty, because he had been "adequately compensated through the terms of his employment."[29] (See also pages 43 and 54–55.)

---

24. Graham v. Scissor-Tail, Inc., 28 Cal. 3d 807, 171 Cal. Rptr. 604, 623 P.2d 165 (1981).

25. *Id.* at 820.

26. *See* note 24 *supra* and Edin v. Jostens, Inc., 343 N.W.2d 691 (Minn. Ct. App. 1981), Continental Casualty Co. v. Knowlton, 305 Minn. 201, 232 N.W.2d 789 (1975), and Ehlers v. Iowa Warehouse Co., 188 N.W.2d 368 (Iowa 1971).

27. 229 Cal. Rptr. 828, 830 (1986).

28. 229 Cal. Rptr. 828, 834 (1986). *See also* Disher v. Fulgoni, 124 Ill. App. 3d 257, 464 N.C. 2d 639 (1984) (employee confidentiality agreement invalid if it is too broad in scope and duration).

29. Cubic Corp. v. Marty, 185 Cal. App. 3d 438 229 Cal. Rptr. 828, 834 (1986); *see also* Chretian v. Donald L. Bren Co., 151 Cal. App. 3d 389, 198 Cal. Rptr. 523 (1984).

A second ground for claiming unenforceability of an employment contract is more specific and more fully developed in legal decisions. It is the doctrine that a covenant in an employment contract will not be enforced if it unduly restricts an employee's rights of personal mobility or his freedom to pursue an occupation.

These questions usually arise in situations where the employee has entered into a contract which contains a postemployment restriction, such as a promise not to compete with the employer after departure. These covenants are generally enforceable only to the extent that they are reasonable in terms of length of time, geographic scope, and subject matter of restriction. (See also pages 54–58 and 62–65.) For example, in *Smith, Batchelder and Rugg v. Foster,* the New Hampshire court refused to enforce a covenant in an employment contract that provided that employee accountants "will not enter into the employ of, or represent in any manner, any person, firm or corporation who or which was a client of the Employer's at any time prior to the termination of this employment" without written approval by the employer.[30] The court determined that this covenant failed a three-part test of reasonableness. A noncompetition covenant is reasonable only if:

1. Its restraint is no greater than needed to protect the employer's interest
2. It does not impose undue hardship on the employee, and
3. It is not injurious to the public interest

The general rule that noncompetition covenants will only be enforced to the extent that they are reasonable has been applied by many different state courts.[31] This rule is based on the need to protect the individual employee and the need to protect the public from monopolies. A California court has summarized the divergent interests of the employer and employee as follows:

> In the employee situation the courts are concerned not solely with the interest of the competing employers, but also with the employee's interest. The interest of the employee in his own mobility and betterment are deemed paramount to the competitive business interest of the employers, where neither the employee nor his new employer has committed any illegal act accompanying the employment change.[32]

The recognition of an interest of employee mobility thus has two important results: one, a judicially enforceable right to override unreasonable postemployment restrictions, and two, a basis for overcoming other excessive interference with employee efforts to seek advancement in a chosen line

---

30. 119 N.H. 679, 406 A.2d 1310 (1979).
31. Annot., 61 A.L.R.3d 397 (1975).
32. Diodes, Inc. v. Franzen, 260 Cal. App. 2d 244, 67 Cal. Rptr. 19 (1968).

of work. It must be noted that this judicially recognized interest is often specifically reinforced by statutes such as the California Business and Professions Code which provides that, with certain exceptions, "every contract by which anyone is restrained from engaging in a lawful profession, trade, or business of any kind is to that extent void."[33]

Adequacy of compensation

In addition to unconscionability and employee mobility, a third ground for claiming unenforceability of an employment contract is inadequacy of consideration. This ground is, however, more problematic. The basic principle is akin to unconscionability: if there is no consideration or inadequate consideration given to the employee for burdens from obligations such as assignment of patent rights or noncompetition covenants, then the promise ought not to be enforced by a court. For example, in a recent case the Minnesota Supreme Court indicated that, to be enforced, a noncompetition clause in a contract should provide the employee with "real advantages."[34]

Real advantages to the employee would probably include increased salary, stock options, or other benefits. They might also include a provision for participation in royalties or other income derived from specific inventions developed by an employee who was obligated to assign invention rights to the employer. In any event, such advantages should be substantial and be in proper proportion to the value of the inventiveness that the employee contributed to the company.

A very good example of the importance of adequate compensation is provided by *Cubic Corporation v. Marty*. In that case an employment contract containing a very forceful provision requiring the employee to disclose and assign discoveries and inventions was enforced by the California court even though the court recognized that the contract was an "adhesion contract." The key factor was the adequacy of the compensation given to the inventive employee, Marty. The evidence in the case showed that Marty had received a substantial raise and had been made a program manager, "in part because of his invention."[35] Marty, the court said, had been "adequately compensated through the terms of his employment." (The case is also discussed on pages 41 and 54–55.)[36]

The California, Illinois, Minnesota, North Carolina, and Washington invention statutes

The problem of inadequate compensation of employee inventors has prompted some states to enact legislation to protect the employees. For

33. CAL. BUS. & PROF. CODE Section 16600 and *see* Section 3.13 *infra*.

34. Freeman v. Duluth Clinic, Ltd., 334 N.W.2d 626, 630 (1983), and *see* Cubic Corp. v. Marty, 185 Cal. App. 3d 438.

35. 229 Cal. Rptr. 828, 831 (1986).

36. *See also* Aetna-Standard Engineering Co. v. Rowland, 493 A.2d 1375 (Pa. Super. 1985), in which it was held that an employee hired as general engineer was not required to assign the patent on his invention to his employer, because he was not specifically compensated to invent.

example, in 1979 a memo seeking support for an "inventor's bill of rights" in California stated:

> The employed inventor usually receives little or nothing in compensation for his efforts. One recent survey found that more than half of the chemical patent holders in California received *a dollar or less* in compensation for their inventions. This situation is not only unfair to the employee but it harms the employer as well by removing any incentive for the worker to invent.[37]

In response to a need for protection of employees, the California legislature adopted a statute in 1979 modeled after one adopted two years earlier in Minnesota.

Limits of invention assignments.   Under the California law an employment contract provision is void if it requires an employee to assign (or offer to assign) to the employer rights to an invention that the employee developed entirely on his or her own time without the employer's supplies, equipment, facilities, or "trade secret information," except for those inventions that either:

1. Relate at the time of conception or reduction to practice to the employer's business, or actual or demonstrably anticipated research or development of the employer *or*

2. Result from *any* work performed by the employee for the employer.[38]

Under this law, a provision in an employment contract in California is invalid to the extent that it attempts to assign inventions to the employer which are solely the product of the employee's time and effort outside of his or her employment assignment. Thus, one corporate officer who opposed the bill complained, "an employee could do his inventing at home and retain rights to all his inventions irrespective of whether they pertain to his employer's business."[39] The employer's response to such a problem, however, is straightforward: The employer should require application of the employee's skills within the context of employment, thus creating an equitable (and legal) basis for a contractual claim to a given invention. (Refer also to pages 52–54.)

It should be noted that the scope of protection to the employee under the California statute may be in practical effect quite limited and fragile.

---

37. Memorandum dated January 15th, 1979 from Assemblyman Terry Goggin to other members of the Assembly regarding his proposed legislation.

38. The California Law, CAL. LAB. CODE 2870–2872, is reproduced in the Appendix. The italics in the text have been added.

39. Letter dated May 25th, 1979 from M. P. Crotty, Vice-President of Rockwell International to Senator Bill Greene. In general accord with this view is an interpretation by Robert L. Gullette in 62 J. PAT. OFF. SOC'Y., 732 at 743 (1980).

A court is permitted to interpret the law to allow a valid employer claim if the invention relates to the employer's business and there has been any use of employer equipment or ideas combined with "any work performed by the employee for the employer."[40] Rarely indeed will the inventive employee's activities be so isolated from his or her job assignment as to be isolated from such a claim.

The Minnesota, Washington, Illinois, and North Carolina laws are substantially similar to California's, with one major difference.[41] Only California law specifies that an employer may require an employee to assign inventions related to the employer's business at the time of conception or reduction to practice of the invention.[42] The other states' laws do not clarify what agreements may be made regarding employee inventions conceived during employment but reduced to practice later.[43]

It has been said that the Washington statute appears to provide greater ownership rights to employers,[44] while the California and Minnesota statutes are intended to encourage innovation outside the field of the employer's business.[45] The differences among the statutes are, however, subtle.

Disclosure of inventions.   A second feature of the California and North Carolina laws is a provision that permits employers to require employees to disclose all inventions "made solely or jointly with others during the term of his or her employment."[46] In California, the employer is obliged to keep the disclosures in confidence; the North Carolina statute imposes no similar restriction.[47] The disclosure is useful to the employer in that it allows the employer to assert claims of ownership based on the contract or on employer trade secrets. The statute authorizes the use of a review process for determining the issues that may arise between the employer and employee with respect to the actual ownership of the work product.

---

40. CAL. LAB. CODE Section 2870.

41. MINN. STAT. ANN. Section 181.78. The Minnesota law is more stringent than California's in that it requires that an invention which is developed with partial use of employer equipment, etcetera, must relate "directly to the business of the employer" if an employer claim is to be made on the basis of relationship to the employer's current business. The Minnesota law was the first of the statutes to be enacted, having been added to the code in 1977.

42. CAL. LAB. CODE Section 2870(a)(1), as amended in July 1986.

43. *Cf.* White's Electronics, Inc. v. Teknetics, Inc., 607 Or. App. 63, 72, 677 P.2d 68 (1984) (employee not required to assign invention conceived while employed by plaintiff but developed later; "he left with an idea and a goal but not an invention").

44. 62 J. PAT. OFF. SOC'Y. 732 at 741 (1980). While there might be nuances of difference to be drawn from the different structure of the Washington Act, I do not find a basis for a substantially different coverage.

45. Coolley, *Recent Changes in Employee Ownership Laws: Employers May Not Own Their Inventions and Confidential Information,* 11 BUS. LAW. 57, 66 (1985).

46. CAL. LAB. CODE Section 2871.

47. *Id.*

The Washington statute also contains a provision which requires employees to "disclose all inventions being developed by the employee, for the purpose of determining employer or employee rights."[48] The Minnesota and Illinois laws are silent on the matter of disclosure of employee inventions; however, there appears to be nothing which would invalidate a reasonable contract provision requiring such disclosure.

Notice of rights.   Under all the state statutes, except North Carolina's, if an employment agreement is entered into after the effective date of the statute and the agreement contains a provision requiring an assignment of invention rights, the employer must notify the employee of his or her rights to limited assignment of inventions as provided by the law. The laws of Minnesota, Illinois, and Washington are more informative in this regard, as they require the employer to inform the employee of the actual legal restrictions in the contract.[49] (For example, the contract might provide: "this agreement does not apply to an invention for which no equipment, supplies, facility, or trade secret information were used..." etc.) California law provides for notice of rights by the cryptic phrase that "the agreement does not apply to an invention which qualifies fully under the provisions of Section 2870." If notice of rights were given in this fashion, the employee would have to demonstrate sufficient curiosity to discover the content of California Labor Code Section 2870.

Burden of proof.   Burden of proof is always critical, as it is an item which both a judge and a jury rely on to see who should prevail in a controversy if the facts and equities are otherwise equal. In California, Washington, North Carolina, and Illinois, the statutes provide that the employee bears the burden of proving that a contract violates the limitations established by the law. The Minnesota act, however, is silent on this point. Given the strong language of the act and its remedial nature, a good argument can be made that the burden rests on the employer to show compliance with the act in Minnesota.

Inventions of anticipated interest to a large employer.   Each of the five statutes has a broad provision which may allow an employer to claim rights if the invention relates to the "employer's actual or demonstrably anticipated research or development." This gives broad scope to certain employer claims under a contract. This is especially true if the employer is a large company with many subdivisions. California has a legislative history which helps confine the scope of such employer claims. The author

---

48. Wash. Rev. Code Section 49.44.150.
49. Minn. Stat. Ann. Section 181.78(3) (1977); Wash. Rev. Code Ann. Section 49.44.140(3) (1979); Ill. Rev. Stat. ch. 140, Section 302(3) (1983).

of the bill stated that the intention was to restrict the meaning of the term "employer" to "the division, affiliate, subsidiary, profit center, or company (whichever unit is the smallest) rather than to the parent corporation."[50]

Cross references. It should be noted that restrictions such as unconscionability (pages 38–39) retain their impact on the contract in addition to the statutes. Also, the "shop right doctrine" may apply to create a nonexclusive or shared right to use the employee's invention[51] (pages 48–52). Furthermore, the restrictions contained in the state law will probably not override federal legal restrictions on federal government employees (pages 70–72).

The following guideline takes into account principles which have been developed in the last four sections.

GUIDELINE THREE

Essential Interests

In keeping with the obligation of good faith, the employer and the employee should take into account both the specific legal requirements related to employment and the essential interests of each party. The employee's interests include: a fair contract, mobility, adequacy of compensation, and fair recognition of invention rights. The employer's interests include: employee loyalty, job performance, preservation of secrets, and fair treatment of the employer's investment of time and energy.

In addition to emphasizing the three guidelines which have been stated so far, I recommend that the components of a good work environment stated on page 4 be reviewed. The three guidelines state the essence of certain critical legal doctrines. The components of a work environment go beyond legal constraints and state essential practical considerations. These practical considerations may also be important in the eyes of a judge or jury, if a situation is litigated. The legal system tends to take into account the overall picture, and the judge or jury is always interested to see "who has the equities," or "what is fair."

---

50. Statement by Assemblyman Goggin to the speaker and members of the Assembly and Senate of the California legislature.

51. The Illinois statute specifically retains employers' shop rights. Ill. Rev. Stat. ch. 140, Section 302(2) (1983).

The resulting property claims

The shop right doctrine

The employment relationship is in fact reciprocal; responsibilities lie with both parties. The reciprocal nature of the relationship has led to the development of the doctrines which we have surveyed so far. The development of law is not a neutral process. The proponents of new legislation or new court decisions seek to advance certain interests or to vindicate certain principles. In the development of employment law we often see a conflict between the employer and the employee in regard to their respective interests and concepts of fairness.[52] The outcome of a struggle between opposing sides depends on the relative political strength of each in the legislative process, prior rulings in court, and on support from fundamental norms such as those found in the Constitution.

One specific area of reciprocity is the interdependence of employer and employee in the inventive process. This interdependence has resulted in the development by the courts of the Shop Right Doctrine.[53] This doctrine recognizes that both the employee and the employer contribute to the inventive process. The contributions are generally:

& The employee contributes individual (or combined) inventiveness, effort, and teamwork.

& The employer contributes facilities, opportunity to collaborate, past accumulated knowledge, and perhaps opportunity.

When these combine to produce something valuable, the employer, the employee, and the public all have claims which courts can recognize. Based on considerations of equity or fairness, the courts have recognized that, in the absence of any statute or contract to the contrary, the employer has a right to a *nonexclusive use* (a shop right) of inventions developed by an employee within the scope of his or her duties.[54] The employee[55] retains

---

52. There is the additional ingredient of service to the overall common good or public interest.

53. The Shop Right Doctrine is a common law doctrine. It has, however, been codified and modified by statute in some states. *See*, for example, CAL. LAB. CODE Section 2860 in the Appendix and discussed on pages 51–52 *infra*.

54. It appears that no court has granted an employee a shop right in his or her employer's patented invention. See Mainland Industries, Inc. v. Timberland Machines and Engineering Corp., 58 Or. App. 585, 649 P.2d 613, petition for review denied, 293 Or. 801, 653 P.2d 999 (1982), cert. denied, 460 U.S. 1051 (1983) and Mislow, *Necessity May Be the Mother of Invention, But Who Gets Custody? The Ownership of Intellectual Property Created by an Employed Inventor*, 1 SANTA CLARA COMP. & HIGH-TECH. L.J. 59, 76 (1985).

55. Shop rights may be owned by the employer of an independent contractor as well. Franklyn v. Guilford Packing Co., 695 F.2d 1158 (9th Cir. 1983).

ownership of invention (for example, a patent if one has been obtained), but the employer has a right to use it without additional compensation.

The determination of whether the employer has a shop right is made based on consideration of several different factors:[56]

1. Whether the invention was developed within the scope of the employee's duties[57]

2. Whether the work on the invention was done during working hours

3. The extent of the use of the employer's resources[58]

4. The relationship of the invention to the employer's business interests[59]

5. Which party (employer or employee) bears the risk of failure[60]

6. The degree to which there was agreement, consent, or acquiescence to use or ownership of the work product

The *United States v. Dubilier Condenser Corp.* illustrates the scope of the Shop Right Doctrine. While working in the radio section of the United States Bureau of Standards, two employees, Dunmore and Lowell, "conceived the idea of using ordinary house-lighting alternating current in the operation of radio apparatus and of means for eliminating hum caused by the alternations of such current." They perfected their process and received three patents from the patent office. Dubilier Condenser Corporation was granted an exclusive license to use these inventions. The United States government then brought a suit in equity, claiming that Dubilier Corporation should be declared a trustee for the United States and required to assign all right, title, and interests in the underlying patents to the government which was the rightful owner.[61] The Supreme Court roundly rejected the government claim of ownership: Dunmore and Lowell had not been employed specifically to invent, thus the invention remained their property. The court emphasized the "reluctance of courts to imply or infer an agreement by the employee to assign his patent." However, the court

---

56. I am pleased to acknowledge the contribution of Ms. Debra Bartle Bristow Esq. in the research and analysis of the scope of the Shop Right Doctrine.

57. United States v. Dubilier Condenser Corp., 289 U.S. 178 (1933), Aero-Bolt and Screw Co. v. Iaia, 180 Cal. App. 2d 728, 5 Cal. Rptr. 53 (1960), Banner Metals v. Lockwood, 178 Cal. App. 2d 643, 3 Cal. Rptr. 421 (1960), Future Craft Corp. v. Clary Corp., 205 Cal. App. 279, 23 Cal. Rptr. 198 (1962), Hollingsworth Solderless Terminal Co. v. Turley, 622 F.2d 1324 (9th Cir., 1980).

58. *Id. See also* Mechmetals Corp. v. Telex Computer Products, Inc., 709 F.2d 1287 (9th Cir. 1983).

59. Dorr-Oliver, Inc. v. United States, 432 F.2d 447 (Ct. Cl. 1970).

60. Gill v. United States, 160 U.S. 426 (1896), Wiegand v. Dover Mfg. Co., 292 F. 255 (N.D. Ohio 1923).

61. United States v. Dubilier Condenser Corp., 49 F.2d 306 (D. Del. 1931).

did recognize that, as conceded by the inventors, the government should enjoy a right to use the inventions without payment of royalty.

The shop right existed in *Dubilier* because the employees had devised and perfected their invention within the course of their employment. They were engaged in devising various improvements for military uses of radio when the inventions at issue were conceived. They were permitted to continue their own work on these inventions in the government laboratory, thus, the employer had participated in the development and a shop right was appropriate.

Banner Metals, Inc. v. Lockwood (178 Cal. App. 2d 643, 3 Cal. Rptr. 421 [1960]) illustrates the normal limit of shop right claims. Lockwood had been employed as a salesman and sales manager for a wire and metal fabricating company. While in their employ he conceived of and developed a useful method of stacking wire receptacles in bakery trucks. He obtained a patent on the device, and the successor to his employer sued him to establish a shop right in the invention. The claim to a shop right was rejected. The trial court had determined that Lockwood's employment duties did not include inventing, that he had conceived and designed the item on his own time and at his own expense, and that he had not used the employer's materials and equipment. The court of appeal ruled that there was no shop right. It emphasized that while Lockwood did have certain responsibilities to design solutions for specific customer problems, he had not been employed for the purpose of providing inventions. The fact that he carried the title of vice-president at the time he conceived the invention and that he used a small amount of company wire (four dollars and twenty cents' worth) did not alter the conclusion. Further, the court noted that Lockwood had disclosed his invention to the employer and the company had expressed no interest at the time.

In computer and high technology situations, the most important single factor favoring the employer's shop right claim is likely to be the contribution from the employer's resources, especially the employer's idea resources. While it is true that the employer cannot claim the right to the fruits of the employee's education or inventiveness, it is also true that the employer has a very firm claim if the invention dependent largely on the research environment in which it was created.

The Shop Right Doctrine is one of equity which has been applied in many different state courts.[62] It is likely that it will be followed in all jurisdictions in appropriate circumstances, that is, where there is no statute or express contract provision which displaces its application.

---

62. *See* the annotation in 61 A.L.R. 2d 356 at Section 7 (1958). *See also* Gemco Eng'r. and Mfg. Co., Inc. v. Henderson, 151 Ohio St. 95, 84 N.E. 2d 596 (1949).

To some extent, California presents a special case with regard to shop rights. In that state, shop rights have been codified.[63] More accurately, they have been subsumed in a statute which declares employer rights:

> Everything which an employee acquires by virtue of his employment, except the compensation which is due him from his employer, belongs to the employer, whether acquired lawfully or unlawfully, or during or after the expiration of the term of his employment (California Labor Code Section 2860).

By its terms the statute is subject to a construction favoring a broader employer claim than the common law doctrine. "Everything acquired by virtue of his employment" might be interpreted to mean anything which is developed in connection with the employment. Such a construction, however, has been rejected.

Two cases elaborating the California approach should be examined.[64] The first is *Williams v. Weisser* (273 Cal. App. 2d 726, 78 Cal. Rptr. 542 [1969]). In the Williams case, UCLA Professor Williams sued the publisher of certain outlines and "canned" class notes. The defendant had hired a UCLA student to sit in on Williams' anthropology class and take notes which were then published under defendant's copyright notice. The court ruled that the property rights in the lectures belonged to the professor. The defendant had argued among other things that the university rather than the plaintiff owned the copyright to the lectures, due to California Labor Code Section 2860. (If this were true, the professor would not be the proper party to sue.) The court rejected the contention: "the code speaks of things which the employee 'acquires,' not matter which he creates."[65]

The second case is *KGB, Inc. v. Giannoulas.* Giannoulas is apparently a talented comic who created a silly character and routine of sideline entertainment at San Diego Padres' baseball games. Giannoulas dressed up in a chicken suit and entertained the audience with his antics. Giannoulas was employed by KGB Radio when he did the routines and made his appearances on behalf of the station as the "KGB Chicken." Giannoulas left the employ of KGB, and it then sued him and obtained an injunction forbidding him from appearing in any chicken costume substantially similar

---

63. See also Ill. REV. STAT. ch. 140, section 302 (2) (1983), reserving common law shop rights of employees.

64. The *Banner Metals* case discussed on page 50 also implicitly deals with CAL. LAB. CODE Section 2860 as it applies and defines California Shop Right Law.

65. 273 Cal. App. 2d 726, 733, 78 Cal. Rptr. 542 (1969). The analysis of why the professor owned the intellectual property would be different now due to the new Copyright Act which replaces a statutory copyright for the common law copyright in unpublished works. *See* pages 15–17 *supra.*

to the KGB chicken costume and from appearing in any chicken suit in any sports event where a San Diego team appears.

The broad scope of the trial court injunction was sharply confined by the court of appeal. Only Giannoulas's appearance in a specifically defined KGB chicken suit could be prevented. Otherwise Giannoulas must remain free to perform and act as a chicken in his own unique way. Labor Code 2860 could not be extended to allow an employer to claim the rights to an entire act, routine, or form of costume. Furthermore, both the First Amendment communication freedoms and the considerations of one's "right to a livelihood" militated against a monopoly on a chicken act.[66]

Rules of interpretation   The *Dubilier* case establishes an analysis which has had, and will have, wide impact on invention rights in the employment context. (See pages 49–50.) While emphasizing that the courts should resist implying or inferring that an employee has assigned away invention rights, the court recognized that the nature of the job assignment may call for implied rights for the benefit of the employer. A specific assignment to invent may lead to an implied assignment of rights:

> One employed to make an invention, who succeeds, during his term of service, in accomplishing that task, is bound to assign to his employer any patent obtained. The reason is that he has only produced that which he was employed to invent.[67]

In addition to the nature of the job assignment, an important consideration is whether the work of invention is done on or off the job. This latter distinction has been elaborated in the Shop Right Doctrine and in the employee invention statutes of California, Illinois, Minnesota, North Carolina, and Washington. Based on these concepts, job assignment and location of invention activity, the following general rules of interpretation of the employment relation can be stated:

1. A job assignment *to invent* implies assignment of the intellectual property right itself (e.g., assignment of patent rights).

2. A job assignment *to design* or improve (as opposed to invent) implies a shop right.

3. A more *generalized job assignment* requiring neither invention nor design tends to imply no employer rights to inventions.

---

66. 104 Cal. App. 3d 844, 856, 164 Cal. Rptr. 571 (1980).
67. United States v. Dubilier Condenser Corp., 289 U.S. 178, 187 (1933). *See also* Speck v. North Carolina Dairy Foundation 311 N.C. 679, 319 S.E. 2d 139, 143 (1984).

4. Work done *on the job* supports a claim of shop right and helps to show implied assignment of invention rights.

5. Work done *off the job* tends to negate employer claims. (See also pages 77–81.)

GUIDELINE FIVE

> **Job Assignments**
> The nature of the job assignment (for example, to invent) and the location where work is done (on the job/off the job) tend to determine claims of ownership of intellectual property rights.

Copyright of "works for hire"

In one particular area, copyrightable material, the implications of one's job assignment loom very large, indeed. The 1978 Copyright Act provides:

> In the case of a work made for hire, the employer or other person for whom the work was prepared is considered the author for purposes of this title, and, unless the parties have agreed otherwise in a written instrument signed by them, owns all the rights comprised in the copyright (17 U.S.C. Section 201[b]).

The act defines a work made for hire as one "prepared by an employee within the scope of his or her employment."[68] In attempting to determine whether a work was prepared within the scope of employment, the courts will examine such factors as the employee's duties, his or her hours and compensation, when and where the work was created, and whether the employer provided supplies.[69] Above all, the courts will consider whether the employer exercised control and supervision over the creation of the work. If the employer did exercise such control, the work is likely to be considered one which was done for hire and which belongs to the employer. If such employer supervision is absent, the employee's claim is likely to be honored.[70]

---

68. 17 U.S.C. Section 101 (1976). A work-for-hire also includes works specifically commissioned from independent contractors if a written instrument designates the work to be for hire. *See* Childers v. High Society Magazine, Inc., 557 F. Supp. 978 (S.D.N.Y. 1983), aff'd. on rehearing, 561 F. Supp. 1374 (S.D.N.Y. 1983).

69. Compare Sygma Photo News, Inc. v. Globe Inter., Inc., 616 F. Supp. 1153 (D.C.N.Y. 1985) (independent photographer working under "gentleman's agreement" with Buckingham Palace to photograph Royal Family held to own copyright) with Peregrine v. Lauren Corp., 601 F. Supp. 828 (D. Col. 1985) (agency controlled and supervised photographer's work and thus owned copyright).

70. Whelan Associates v. Jaslow Dental Labor., 609 F. Supp. 1307 (D.C. Pa.

Invention provisions in contracts

"The respective rights and obligations of employer and employee, touching an invention conceived by the latter, spring from the contract of employment."[71] Employment contracts frequently cover the ownership of inventions and ownership of the creation of ideas. Three examples of contract provisions follow.

1. One agreement provides that the employee agrees to disclose and assign all "inventions, improvements, data, processes, computer software programs, and discoveries that are conceived or made by me alone or with others while I am employed . . . "

2. Another provides that the employee does "hereby assign my entire right, title and interest in any idea, invention, design of a useful article (whether the article is ornamental or otherwise), computer program and related documentation, and other work of authorship hereafter made or conceived solely or jointly by me . . . " The assignment covers all such ideas and works that either relate to actual or anticipated interests of the employer or which are "suggested by" any assigned task done for the employer. In the case of copyright, the assignment is only as to items which are both related to employer interests and suggested by assigned tasks.

3. A third provides that the employee agrees to give the employer "full benefit and enjoyment of any and all inventions or improvements which he may make while in the employ of R relating to methods, apparatus, chemical substances, or methods of producing which are being used, manufactured or developed by R, or the use, manufacture and development of which was at the time of said invention or inventions in contemplation by R and all inventions which are made or worked out on the time and at the expense of R."

Each of these three formulations is intended to have a broad sweep and to secure for the employer the rights to ownership of the idea work. The first of these provisions is a type that requires the employee to disclose and assign inventions. A provision of this type was enforced against the employee in *Cubic Corporation v. Marty*. In that case, the employee, Marty, had signed a contract which required him

---

1985); Epoch Producing Corp. v. Killiam Shows, Inc., 522 F.2d 737, 744 (2d Cir., 1975), Picture Music, Inc. v. Bourne, Inc., 457 F.2d 1213 (2d Cir., 1972) and Cory Van Arsdale, *Computer Programs and Other Faculty Writings Under the Work for Hire Doctrine*, 1 COMPUTER AND TECHNOLOGY L.J. (1984).

71. United States v. Dubilier Condenser Corp., 289 U.S. 178, 187 (1933). See pages 35–38.

To promptly disclose to Company all ideas, processes, inventions, improvements, developments and discoveries coming within the scope of Company's business or related to Company's products or to any research, design experimental or production work carried on by Company, or to any problems specifically assigned to Employee, conceived alone or with others during this employment, and whether or not conceived during regular working hours.[72]

After entering employment, Marty conceived of an idea that he then presented to his employer. The employer then funded a project to study the invention and Marty was given "a substantial raise in salary and made a program manager."[73] The contract provision was enforced against Marty, and his employer was granted rights to the patent and $34,000 damages against Marty after he had defied the employer's claim under the contract and had refused to assign a patent that he had obtained for the invention. Marty was also enjoined from exploiting any rights under his patent and from "using or disclosing Cubic's confidential information to others." The *Cubic* case illustrates the importance of examining and abiding by terms of a contract that has been fairly compensated. In that case the court had reviewed the terms of the contract and found them to be fair to the employee.

The third of these provisions has had a judicial interpretation which has sharply confined its scope and which awarded the inventions at stake to the employee. *Jamesbury Corporation v. Worchester Valve Company* (318 F. Supp. 1 [D. Mass. 1970]) was a case involving a valuable hydraulic valve which had been invented and patented by Freeman, the former director of research for the Rockwood Sprinkler Company.[74] Freeman's employment contract with Rockwood contained the precise language of example number 1 above. The successor company to Rockwood claimed the rights to the invention based on the contract. The court found that Freeman had conceived the ideas of the invention and had gained the technical knowledge necessary to develop it while he was in Rockwood's employ. The court determined that "Freeman knew very well what he was going to do" with his discovery before he left Rockwood. He had contacted a friend, obtained commitments from investors, and hired an attorney to draft Articles of Incorporation to set up a company to exploit the ideas. Despite this chain of events, the contract claim for "the full benefit and enjoyment of any and all inventions" made while employed was denied.

The denial of the claim by the former employer's legal successor was based on the contract itself. The court noted that the contract language gave the employer a right only to inventions, not ideas. Under Massachusetts law, applied in the case, an idea does not become an invention until

---

72. 229 Cal. Rptr. 828, 830 (1986).
73. 229 Cal. Rptr. 828, 833 (1986).
74. Aff'd., 443 F.2d 205 (1st Cir., 1971).

it is reduced to some tangible form.[75] Freeman knew what he wanted to do, that is, go out on his own. Thus, by deliberately refraining from reducing his ideas to drawings or other tangible form, he protected his ideas against the contractual claim. He took no trade secret and abused no confidence and was therefore entitled to patent rights.[76]

The other two contract examples were more inclusive in their scope. "Discoveries" (example 1) and "ideas" (example 2) are covered by these provisions. Thus, by their terms, they would allow the employer to claim all of the idea work product developed in accordance with the rest of the contract terms.[77]

The idea or invention provisions in employment contracts are subject to rules limiting their effectiveness and scope. Like other parts of the contract they are subject to the limits of unconscionability, employee rights of mobility, arguments concerning adequacy of compensation, and the specific requirements of certain state laws. Assuming the contract provision is not invalid or unenforceable, it will nevertheless be subject to the following legal arguments regarding its scope:

1. The claims will be limited to the terms of the contract itself. This is exemplified by the *Jamesbury* case, discussed previously.

2. The provisions of the contract may not be enforced if they are too vague.[78]

3. The invention or idea provision will be interpreted in a manner consistent with the actual behavior of the parties.

4. The provisions will be likely "to be construed somewhat strictly against the employer."[79]

5. Such provisions are arguably subject to a reasonable scope limitation. This is very similar to the limitation which exists as to noncompetition clauses. See the following discussion on pages 62–65.

The last two limitations, strict construction and a limit of reasonable scope, have not been fully tested in courts. It is predictable that there will be much litigation concerning these points in the future. At this point we

---

75. *See also* pages 3–4 and 7–8 *supra.*

76. *See also* Andreaggi v. Relis, 171 N.J. Super. 203, 408 A.2d 455 (1979) and White's Electronics v. Teknetics, Inc., 67 Or. App. 63, 677 P.2d 68 (1984).

77. Jamesbury Corp. v. Worcester Valve Co., 443 F.2d 205, 211 (1st Cir., 1971) and Winston Research Corp. v. Minnesota Mining and Mfg. Co., 350 F.2d 134 (9th Cir., 1965).

78. Seach v. Richards, Dieterle and Co., 439 N.E.2d 208 (Ind. Ct. App. 1982).

79. Jamesbury Corp. v. Worcester Valve Co., 318 F. Supp. 1, 8 (D. Mass. 1970) and *see* Monsanto Chemical Works v. Jaeger, 31 F.2d 188, 191 (W.D. Pa. 1929), and DeCristofaro v. Security Nat'l. Bank, 664 P.2d 167 (Alaska, 1983).

should examine some of the precedents that form the basis for these arguments limiting the scope of contract provisions.

In *Aspinwall Manufacturing Co. v. Gill* (32 F. 697 [D.N.J. 1887]), the inventor of a patented potato planter sued certain others for infringement of his patent. Relief was denied to the inventor because the allegedly infringing planters were actually improved versions of a prior model to which the inventor had assigned rights to the defendants. In the course of the opinion the court had occasion to recognize that an assignment of rights to future improvements of a specific invention should be given legal effect. However, the court continued:

> A naked assignment or agreement to assign, in gross, a man's future labors as an author or inventor—in other words, a mortgage on a man's brain, to bind all its future products—does not address itself favorably to our consideration.[80]

Despite the precautionary rule stated in *Aspinwall*, contracts granting the employer the right to the employee's future inventions have been sustained. Undoubtedly one of the leading cases in favor of the employer's point of view is *Goodyear Tire and Rubber Company v. Miller* (22 F.2d 353 [9th Cir., 1927]). In that case, the defendant inventor had been employed in a machine design department of Goodyear and had signed a contract by which he agreed to disclose "any and all inventions" which he might make during the term of his employment or within one year after termination. Based upon the agreement, the tire rotating machine which he developed during the employment and at Goodyear's premises was determined to be the property of Goodyear. The court also emphasized that the result should have been the same absent the specific contract, because his work had been "exclusively in a department, the function of which was to improve old and discover new processes and devices."[81] The result in the *Goodyear* case, enforcement of a specific provision to assign inventions, has been qualified in some subsequent cases to take into account the restrictions suggested by the *Aspinwall* case: the courts ought not to enforce "a mortgage on a man's brain." In *Guth v. Minnesota Mining and Manufacturing Company* (72 F.2d 385 [7th Cir., 1934]), it was argued that a chemical engineer who had worked for 3M had invented a process and should be obliged to sign a patent application on behalf of 3M. In determining the issues presented, the court examined the engineer's employment contract which provided that he was obliged to assign all inventions in which the employer or its successor "is or may be concerned" and all inventions that he may "hereafter make or conceive." The court acknowledged that the

---

80. 32 F. 697, 700 (D.N.J. 1887) and *see* Eastern Dynamite Co. v. Keystone Powder Mfg. Co., 164 F. 47, 50 (M.D. Pa. 1908).

81. 22 F.2d 353, 356 (9th Cir., 1927) and *see* pages 52–53.

engineer had been employed for the purpose to do research. Nevertheless, it found that the contract "conflicts with the public policy of the land." The court stated:

> Upon the facts peculiar to this case we are convinced that those provisions of the contract which were limitless in extent of time and in subject matter of invention were contrary to public policy. Guth was a chemical engineer. He was more or less successful in research work, as is shown by the fact basis of this litigation. He was a research man prepared to devote his life to discoveries of value to industry. Under this contract he was, however, if he worked in another laboratory or for another manufacturer, required to assign his discoveries to appellee. This would effectively close the doors of employment to him. Until the end of the chapter he was compelled either to work for appellee or turn over the children of his inventive genius to it. Such a contract conflicts with the public policy of the land, which is one that encourages inventions and discourages the exclusion of an employee from engaging in the gainful occupation for which he is particularly fitted for all time, anywhere in the United States.[82]

It is probably agreed that these cases do establish certain limits on the scope of invention agreements. First, the agreement to assign inventions must bear some relation to the employer's actual or anticipated business.[83] Second, provisions which claim inventions made after employment has ceased should only be enforced if the carry-over period is reasonable and necessary.[84] Beyond this it is not clear to what extent the content of invention provisions will be reviewed by courts to determine whether they are reasonable in scope. It is my view that it is likely that courts will be willing to review such agreements and to confine their scope to that which is actually necessary to protect the employer's investment in development. Furthermore, protection of the employer's interest will be granted only to the extent that the employee's interest in mobility and betterment are also preserved.[85]

Confidentiality obligations   The employer has the right to retain and control all those items which constitute its property. Thus, the employer can obtain legal protection for the expressions and processes which are copyrighted, patented, protected as trade secrets or trademarks, or which had specifically recognized attributes of confidentiality, such as customer lists.[86]

---

82. 72 F.2d 385, 388 (7th Cir., 1934).
83. Knoth, *Assignment of Future Inventions*, 27 CHI.-KENT L. REV., 295, 299 (1949).
84. *See* Ingersoll-Rand Co. v. Ciavetti, 509 A.29 821 (N.J. Super. Ch. 1986); Dorr-Oliver, Inc. v. United States, 432 F.2d 447, 452 (Ct. Cl. 1970).
85. For a contrary opinion, *see* Knoth, note 60.
86. *See* Chapter 2 for a discussion of these forms of intellectual property.

> ## Employer's Property
> The employee must not appropriate the employer's copyrights, patents, trade secrets, trademarks, customer lists, or other clearly preserved confidences.

Cases are legion which reaffirm the employee's obligation not to disclose the employer's trade secrets.[87] The rule is hard and fast, and an outright taking of a secret will be subject to the full range of judicial remedies.[88] There are, however, numerous instances in which the situation will not be one of a clear taking of a secret. The following kinds of questions arise to complicate the application of the rule:

1. Was there a trade secret?
2. Was the fact of secrecy brought home to the employee?
3. If no secret was divulged, does the employer have another basis for insisting on confidentiality?
4. What is the effect of a specific contract provision requiring nondisclosure?

Was there a trade secret? As we have seen, trade secret protection depends entirely on the maintenance of secrecy.[89] Furthermore, no one can claim common processes or knowledge as being the subject of a trade secret. Reverse engineering of a product and use of the discoverable processes (which are not patented or copyrighted) is perfectly legitimate.[90]

Jostens, Inc. v. National Computer Systems (318 N.W. 2d 691 [Minn. 1982]) provides a case in point. In *Jostens* an extremely valuable CAD/CAM process was at issue. Among other things, the plaintiff claimed that the defendant, a former employee and engineer, had appropriated trade secrets when he took his knowledge of a CAD/CAM system for designing jewelry rings to a new, competing employer. The employee, Titus, had worked for Jostens as an engineer, had designed the CAD/CAM system for the company, and had signed an agreement not to disclose information concerning Jostens' business to others. He took his knowledge to a competitor and went right to work on the very same system for the new

---

87. An annotation at 30 A.L.R.3d 631 collects many such cases. *See also* Henry Hope X-Ray Prods., Inc. v. Marron Carrel, Inc., 674 F.2d 1336 (9th Cir., 1982), F.M.C. Corp. v. Varco Int'l., Inc., 677 F.2d 500 (5th Cir., 1982), Jostens, Inc. v. Nat'l. Computer Systems, 318 N.W.2d 691 (Minn. 1982).

88. *See* page 28.

89. *See* pages 23–24.

90. *See* pages 31–32.

employer. The Supreme Court ruled that Titus had not misappropriated trade secrets.

The primary weakness in Jostens' claim was failure to show that they, in fact, created and preserved a trade secret. Titus took with him to the new employer his abilities, his knowledge of computer programming in general, and "his experience and skills acquired while working at Jostens." These items, however, do not constitute trade secrets. As to the explicit material, the CAD/CAM process itself, the company did have a very good, even traditional claim of a trade secret subject matter.[91] The process was undeniably valuable. It had been developed by sustained effort, and it provided a distinct competitive edge, but Jostens had *failed* to keep it secret. Among other things, Jostens had allowed the process to enter the public domain by a presentation which Titus had been permitted to make at a trade conference and by an article he had been permitted to publish in a technical journal.

A second Minnesota case, *Electro-craft Corp. v. Controlled Motion, Inc.* (332 N. W. 2d 890 [Minn. 1983]) provides further clarification of trade secret law. In this case, Mahoney, a former employee of Electro-craft Corporation, set up a new company, Controlled Motion (CMI), to make servo motors in competition with his former employer.[92] Mahoney took steps to set up his new company before he left Electro-craft. These included contacts with four knowledgeable Electro-craft employees who sooned joined CMI. Electro-craft swiftly went to court, suing Mahoney and CMI within six weeks of Mahoney's departure and within ten days of the departure of the other employees. All of these employees, including Mahoney, had signed employment agreements prohibiting them from using or disclosing "any secret or confidential information, knowledge, or data of the employer" without prior written consent. Electro-craft claimed that Mahoney had misappropriated trade secrets and that he and CMI improperly copied the designs of the servo motors. The trial court found in favor of Electro-craft and enjoined CMI. The Supreme Court of Minnesota reversed on the basis that no trade secrets had been misappropriated.[93]

The reasons for a reversal of the trial court were set forth in a two-step process. First of all, the court stated that a showing of the existence of a confidential relationship helps support a claim of violation of trade secret rights, but is not sufficient in itself to establish the existence of a secret.

---

91. *See* pages 24–25.

92. A servo motor is a high performance electric motor whose prime characteristic is the ability to start and stop rapidly. They are used in computer disc drives and other applications requiring speed.

93. A contempt order against the defendants was sustained, however, because the defendants had gone ahead and violated the order rather than obtain a modification.

This is because trade secrets do not include all confidential information, but only those items of information which have been sufficiently protected as such. In other words, the confidential information must be segregated and turned into a specific and identified "idea property" before it can be protected. "Without a proven trade secret there can be no action for misappropriation, even if the defendant's actions were wrongful."[94] In order to find a misappropriation, the court must first find "property" as opposed to confidences alone.

The second step was to search the record for a specific showing of the existence of secrets (as opposed to confidences standing alone). Applying the Uniform Trade Secret Act,[95] the court sustained the lower court's finding that the Electro-craft servo motor information was not generally known, was unique, and had independent economic value. However, Electro-craft had not shown sufficient efforts to maintain secrecy. Security vis-à-vis outsiders was lax. The company failed to let its own employees "know in no uncertain terms" what features were in fact secret. Thus, the claim foundered on lack of protection.[96]

Was the fact of secrecy brought home to the employees? Both the *Jostens* case and the *Electro-craft* case emphasize the importance of whether the employer has informed the employee of what is claimed as secret information. In *Jostens* the court said, "the employee is entitled to fair notice of the confidential nature of the relationship and what material is to be kept confidential." The Electro-craft case followed that emphasis. Although the employees had signed confidentiality agreements, the court found that the employer had not let them know what was really secret. The company had utilized exit interviews,[97] but these were shown to be "little more than attempts to intimidate or threaten employees" and prevent them from leaving and engaging in legitimate competition. These would not qualify as the necessary "ongoing efforts to maintain the secrecy of specific information." The court added that in this regard it would neither condone nor reward the employer's conduct.[98]

If no secret was divulged, does the employer have another basis for insisting on confidentiality? The Minnesota cases give strong indication that without a showing of misappropriation of a specific trade secret, courts should not establish liability against former employees.

---

94. 332 N.W.2d 890, 901 (1983). *See also* Dynamics Research Corp. v. Analytic Sciences Corp., 9 Mass Ap. Ct. 254, 400 N.E.2d 1274 (1980), and Diodes, Inc. v. Franzen, 260 Cal. App. 2d 244, 67 Cal. Rptr. 19 (1968).

95. The Minnesota version of the Uniform Trade Secret Act is set forth in the Appendix.

96. *See also* pages 26–28.

97. *See* pages 26–28.

98. 332 N.W.2d 890, 903 (Minn. 1983).

Nevertheless, are there instances where an employee has played fast and loose with general information or has abused his or her position of confidence so that liability should be imposed? Probably so. *Jostens*, for example, emphasized that employees "have a common law duty not to wrongfully use confidential information or trade secrets obtained from an employer."[99] If an employee occupies a position of trust or confidence, the courts are likely to be quick to protect the employer if it is shown that the employee preferred his or her self-interest to that of the employer. For example, a director of research should not be permitted to turn critical discoveries or a market timing to his own advantage at the expense of the organization for which he works. This restriction is an element of the obligations of good faith and loyalty.[100]

What is the effect of a specific contract provision requiring non-disclosure?   These provisions are extremely important for two reasons. First, they should clarify that there is an obligation not to disclose. Thus, they stand as an initial warning to the employee that there may be items to protect. Second, these contractual provisions may help clarify what it is that the employee should guard. They may do so by emphasizing the elements of the job description or by identifying the type of activity which is sensitive.

It should be emphasized, however, that even a carefully drafted employment contract provision may fail to secure an employer's legitimate interest in non-disclosure, if the employer fails to continue to identify the actual trade secrets and the particular demands of confidentiality. Without such guidance, the employee has simply no basis for determining when to keep silent.

Postemployment covenants   The invention and nondisclosure provisions of the employment contract usually have effects that carry over after the employment terminates. Thus, they are in a real sense postemployment covenants. In addition, there is a species of covenant which is specifically intended to bind the employee after he or she leaves employment. This is the noncompetition covenant. These covenants are generally enforceable only to the extent they are reasonable.[101]

Here are some examples of noncompetition covenants:

---

99. 318 N.W.2d 691, 701 (Minn. 1982).

100. *See* pages 37–38 and Science Accessories Corp. v. Summagraphics Corp., 425 A.2d 957 (Del. 1980), Maryland Metals, Inc. v. Metzner, 282 Md. 31, 382 A.2d 564 (1978), Wexler v. Greenberg, 399 Pa. 569, 160 A.2d 430 (1960), Diodes, Inc. v. Franzen, 260 Cal. App. 2d 244, 67 Cal. Rptr. 19 (1968) and Lear Siegler, Inc. v. Ark-Ell Springs, Inc., 569 F.2d 286, 289 (5th Cir., 1978).

101. *See also* pages 54–58.

1. For one year following any termination of employment the employee will not engage in or enter the employ of or have any interest in, directly or indirectly, any other person, firm, corporation, or other entity engaged in activities relating to lawn and garden care within any geographic area where the employer does business within the period of the employee's employ.[102]

2. I further agree that I will not for a period of two years after the period of my employment by the Company, directly or indirectly in any capacity (whether as owner, partner, shareholder, agent, employee, consultant or otherwise) engage in any business which is or may be similar to or become competitive with the business now or at any time during the course of my employment conducted by the Company anywhere within the United States of America. In making the foregoing agreement, I acknowledge and confirm that the business of the Company is nationwide in scope, that customers and potential customers of the Company are located throughout the United States of America, that the location of the Company's office or offices is not a relevant factor in determining the market area for the Company's product and services, and accordingly, that the Company would be irreparably harmed if I were to compete with the Company anywhere within the United States of America within the prescribed period.[103]

3. For a period ending one year after the end of my employment with A Company, I shall not either directly or indirectly, as proprietor, principal, agent, employee, consultant, or lender become associated with X, Y, or Z Company, or any other person, firm, corporation or other entity which manufactures, sells, or otherwise deals in computer peripheral card readers, nor shall I solicit, canvas or accept, or authorize any person or entity to solicit, canvas or accept from customers of A Company any business related to said readers.[104]

The general rule of reasonableness that governs such covenants is based on the recognition of legitimate interests of both the employer and employee. For example, the employer may wish to protect business goodwill, a relative market advantage, business contracts, or certain information. The employee, on the other hand, wishes to be free to move and practice his or her craft.

---

102. Weed Eater, Inc. v. Dowling, 562 S.W.2d 898, 900 (Tex. Civ. App. 1978).
103. J. C. Matlock, Jr. v. Data Processing Security, Inc., 618 S.W.2d 327 (Tex. 1981).
104. Peripheral Dynamics, Inc. v. Holdsworth, 254 Pa. Super Ct. 310, 385 A.2d 1354 (1978).

There are several areas in which the reasonableness of noncompetition covenants is tested:

Time limits. "In order to be enforceable, the restrictive covenant must contain a reasonable time limitation."[105] Reasonableness of the time limit is judged by such factors as: its relation to preserving employer confidences, customer contacts and goodwill, the impact on employee interests such as mobility, and the overall impact on the public.

Geographic scope. To be reasonable the covenant must usually contain a limitation as to its territorial scope which is reasonably related to the employer's interests. If there is no geographic restriction specified, the courts will sometimes supply one.[106] Courts in some states will not imply limits where none is specified and will simply rule the contract provision is invalid.[107] Even a very large geographic scope may in some instances be ruled reasonable. In *Weed Eater, Inc. v. Dowling* (562 S.W.2d 898 [Tex. Civ. App. 1978]), a restrictive covenant which specified a one-year limit, but no geographic scope, was enforced because the employee's knowledge was so complete that it would permit a new competitor to set up business immediately. The employee was restrained from continuing to work for a Hawaii-based competitor after leaving his Texas-based former employer. The geographic scope was not unreasonable because of the nationwide market for weed trimming devices.

Adequacy of consideration. Noncompetition covenants are often reviewed as to whether the employee is sufficiently compensated for the promise not to compete. Some courts have decided that the employer's grant of continued employment is adequate recompense in itself.[108] Others have said that the employer must provide some adequate additional compensation for such a promise, unless the covenant was contained in the original employment arrangement. "In other words, a restrictive covenant is enforceable if supported by new consideration either in the form of an initial employment contract or a change in the conditions of employment."[109] In states where the court looks at the adequacy of consideration, it is likely that the judge will make some comparison of what the employee gives up with what he or she receives in return. Such items as a leave of absence,

---

105. 41 A.L.R.2d 15, 46 (1955).

106. *See* 43 A.L.R.2d 94 at Sections 7 and 11 (1955). For example, courts following New York law have implied geographic limits where the contract specifies none. Award Incentives, Inc. v. Van Rooyen, 263 F.2d 173 (3d Cir., 1959).

107. For example, MacIntosh v. Brunswick Corp., 241 Md. 24, 215 A.2d 222 (1965).

108. For example, Reed, Roberts Assoc., Inc. v. Bailenson, 537 S.W.2d 238 (Mo. Ct. App. 1976); and *see* 51 A.L.R. 3d 825, Section 4(b).

109. Maintenance Specialties, Inc. v. Gottus, 455 Pa. 327, 314 A.2d 279 (1974). *See* the annotation in 51 A.L.R.3d 825.

a promotion, or profit participation are likely to be viewed as adequate. In *Bradford v. New York Times Company* (501 F.2d 51 [2d Cir., 1974]), the court held that the *New York Times* was entitled to terminate a former general manager's incentive compensation benefits when he became employed by a competitor. Bradford was subject to a ten-year, noncompetition clause. Given the nature of his former position and the business of the *Times*, the court determined that "the time fixed, ten years, is commensurate with the payment of benefits."

Per se invalidity. Employers must take great care when utilizing a covenant not to compete since, in addition to the rule of reasonable restriction, such covenants may be viewed as suspect or even invalid by their very nature. These results are often brought about by state statutes. For example, California Business and Professions Code Section 16600 provides that "every contract by which anyone is restrained from engaging in a lawful profession, trade, or a business of any kind is to that extent void," unless the transaction is permitted by a specific exception, such as a sale of goodwill of a business. Based on this statute, covenants not to compete are invalid "except where their enforcement is necessary to protect the trade secrets of the employer."[110] Other states with similar statutes include Alabama, Michigan, North Dakota, and Oklahoma.[111] It is essential to check the current statutes of the state involved whenever there is a question of the validity of an employee-restrictive covenant or noncompetition clause. If a statute such as California's Business and Professions Code Section 16600 exists, it may make all the difference in the impact of such contractual provisions.

In addition to contract terms, laws, and public policy, the employment relationship is governed by rules set by the employer or by the employer in conjunction with an employee bargaining unit or union. These rules usually embrace such things as working hours, job assignments, and lines of authority. Often they are generated ad hoc and exist in the form of memos and written or unwritten customs. At other times the employer may develop an employee manual or handbook which is intended to contain some of the more important guidelines.

These rules developed within the employment setting may have an important impact on intellectual property claims. They may indicate trade secret practices or define job assignments in ways that tend to establish intellectual property rights. Since this is the case, it is important for the employee to be aware of the elements of his or her employment rules that

Employee handbooks and rules

---

110. Muggill v. Reuben H. Donnelley Corp., 62 Cal. 2d 239, 398 P.2d 147 (1965), Gordon Termite Control v. Terrones, 84 Cal. App. 3d 176, 148 Cal. Rptr. 310 (1978).

111. *See* 3 A.L.R.2d 522 (1955) and 13 A.L.R.4th 661 (1982).

may have an impact on intellectual property claims.[112] It is equally important for the employer to be careful and sensible about the content of its rules, as they will be subject to judicial inquiry and interpretation along the same lines as the employment contract itself.

One large company whose business is primarily the creation and marketing of computers and other intellectual property-based technology has assembled many of its rules and policies in a thirty-page handbook called "Business Conduct Guidelines." This pamphlet is heavily laden with "proprietary information" policies. Here are some items contained in that pamphlet.

1. Part I of the pamphlet is introduced as dealing "primarily with matter arising from your employment relationship . . . it deals with some of your key responsibilities in matters of security, use of (employer) property and recording and reporting information."

2. On page 10 the manual states that the employee assigns to the employer "the right to any ideas and inventions that you develop if they are in an area of the company's business." It states that an employee may ask the company for a written disclaimer of ownership if the employee believes that the invention falls outside company interest. The pamphlet states that ownership of intellectual property created during employment "continues after you leave the company." It states that the company has experienced instances where its "intellectual property has been appropriated or misused." It notes that the company has taken legal actions in the past. "Also, a number of individuals, including former (company) employees, have been prosecuted by government authorities and convicted of crimes for their part in stealing information."

3. Part III of the pamphlet is entitled "On Your Own Time" and deals with potential conflicting interests which the employee may confront. This section contains many sensible guidelines: do not compete with the employer; do not accept money for your services from suppliers; and do not solicit business while on company premises or company time. The guidelines acknowledge that "not every activity on your own time that could conceivably conflict with (the employer's) interests is prohibited." However, the pamphlet indicates that because of the rapid development in the computer area, the company must "draw and redraw lines as new

---

112. Certain terms contained in a policy manual, for example a description of termination procedure, may also create rights enforceable by the employee. Kaiser v. Dixon, 127 Ill. App. 3d 251, 468 N.E.2d 822, 831 (1984). *See also* Woolley v. Hoffmann-LaRoche, Inc., 99 N.J. 284, 491 A.2d 1257 (1985) and Gates v. Life of Montana Ins. Co., 668 P.2d 213 (Mont. 1983).

patterns of activity develop." To find definitive answers, the employee is advised to consult the company management or company legal counsel. The pamphlet does not suggest that the employee may consult independent advisors or legal counsel, nor does it point out employee rights such as mobility or rights to specific notice of company secrets.

It is advisable for the employee to review his or her employment rules in order to be able to act appropriately. It is also appropriate for the employee to raise questions concerning the fairness or even legality of certain stated policies. If the employee is on the track of developing something he feels he has a right to keep, then an outside advisor should be consulted.

From the employer's point of view, it is important to review the adequacy and fairness of the rules governing employees. Steps should be taken, for example, to give notice of the essential secrets so those will not be lost. The employer will also be better served to draft guidelines that take into account the needs of a good work environment. (See page 4.)

Remedies for breach

To the extent that the employment contract and its related obligations are valid, it may be enforced. Validity is determined by reference to the limitations which have been discussed previously in this chapter. When an employer claims that an employee has breached his or her employment obligations relative to idea products, the employer will often also claim that some element of its own intellectual property such as a trade secret has been misappropriated. The possible remedies for the employer include injunctions and damages.

The employee may also cross complain against the employer for breach of any obligations which the employee owes him, as well. These employee claims include interference with the individual's right to pursue a calling.[113] These countervailing claims by the employee should be seriously examined in the event that a legal action is commenced. In this section, however, we will concentrate on the remedies available to the employer and limitations on those remedies.

Specific performance. There are generally two kinds of remedies available in court. One of these is money damages or its equivalent, such as a royalty award. The second is a full range of court orders, including injunctions and specific performance. Specific performance is a court order that one perform his or her contractual obligations. As a general rule, courts will not order specific performance of a contract unless the complaining party can show that damages are an inadequate remedy. Furthermore, it is the general rule by court decision or statute that courts

---

113. Pearson, James O., *Liability for Interference with At Will Business Relationship*, 5 A.L.R. 4th 9. *See also* pp. 42–43.

will not order an employee to perform personal services under an employ-ment contract.[114] "It is clear that no court will order an employee or other person who is to render personal services to perform."[115] Therefore, spe-cific performance is not available to compel an employee to perform invention tasks. On the other hand, specific performance may be available to compel delivery of inventions which have actually been created. For example, it might be clearly demonstrated that the employee was obliged by contract to produce a particular item, say a computer program, and that program or a portion of it has been produced. Under those circumstances, a court might order delivery of the item or completed portion of it to the employer. The court should not, however, order the employee to complete the work.

Injunctions.   Other forms of equity relief may be available. First of all, courts will protect trade secrets by issuing injunctions against their misappropriation.[116] Second, in certain limited circumstances, courts may enjoin an employee who violates a restrictive provision of an employment contract, such as a noncompetition clause, from working for someone else. This may have a practical effect similar to a court order specifically to perform the original employment, because, by forcing the employee out of the job market, it presses him back to work for the original employer. To qualify for such relief, the employer must show irreparable injury and inadequacy of damages as a remedy. The decisions which have granted such relief appear to be primarily ones concerning professional athletes and entertainers.[117] In such cases the employer can readily demonstrate the talent or uniqueness of the performer. If such uniqueness can be shown with respect to an inventive employee, perhaps the employer could obtain an injunction against other competing employment. The strong policy fa-voring employee mobility militates against such a result, however.[118] The employer is also subject to equitable defenses including *laches* (delay), and unclean hands or unfairness on its part.

Damages.   If an employee misappropriates the employer's trade se-crets, copyrights, or patents he or she is subject to liability for damages. The measure of recovery for the employer can be based on a variety of different formulas: the employer's loss of profits, the cost of remedial efforts, the amount of the defendant-employee's gain, or a reasonable roy-

---

114. California Civil Code 3390 and 3423; American Broadcasting Co. Inc. v. Wolf, 52 N.Y.2d 394, 438 N.Y.S. 2d 482 (1981).

115. CALAMARI & PERILLO, THE LAW OF CONTRACTS (SECOND), 585 (1977).

116. *See* Johnson, William F., Jr., *Remedies In Trade Secret Litigation*, 72 N.W.L. Rev. 1004 (1978) and 38 A.L.R.3d 572.

117. MCA Records, Inc. v. Newton-John, 90 Cal. App. 3d 18, 153 Cal. Rptr. 153 (1979), Washington Capitals Basketball Club v. Barry, 419 F.2d 472 (9th Cir., 1969), and Houston Oilers v. Neely, 361 F.2d 36 (10th Cir., 1966).

118. *See* pages 42–43.

alty for the use of the trade secret.[119] In some cases it has been held that the plaintiff may elect the method of assessing damages that provides the greatest recovery.[120]

The employer may be entitled to damages for the loss of the employee's services. If such a claim is made, it should be restricted to those amounts which are definite and which necessarily follow from the breach. For example, if the employee has left the employer and has made use of the employer's trade secrets to his own advantage, the employee should nevertheless be entitled to show which portion of the profit gained is due to the use of the trade secrets and restrict the employer's claim to that.[121]

Consultants

In many phases of intellectual property development individuals are hired as independent contractors or "consultants" rather than engaged as employees. Whether one is an "employee" or a "consultant" may be a very important consideration in determining intellectual property rights. Generally, if one really is an independent contractor rather than an employee, it is more likely that the terms of the contract will determine the respective rights of the company and the consultant without reference to implied terms or other "equities."[122] This is because an independent contract is more often viewed as a fully arm's length transaction.[123] The doctrines of good faith, unconscionability and confidentiality still have powerful roles to play, but they will not be interpreted in the broader context of the overall "relationship" which constitutes employment. (Refer to the earlier discussion on these doctrines.)

The important inquiry may be whether the relationship is in fact independent contractor or whether it is actually employment. That determination will be made based on the following types of factors:

1. Does the person work at his own direction and discretion?

2. Has he or she undertaken the risk of success or failure?

3. Is he or she free to seek other parallel "employment" or activity?

4. Is the intent of the parties to leave the worker independent?

119. *See* 11 A.L.R. 4th 12, *Proper Measure and Elements of Damage for Misappropriation of Trade Secrets.*

120. *Ibid.*

121. *See* Sheldon v. Metro-Goldwyn Meyer Pictures Corp., 390 U.S. 390 (1939), Lugosi v. Universal Pictures, 25 Cal. 3d 813, 855–856, 603 P.2d 425 (1979), Leigh v. Ingle, 727 F.2d 113, 138 (1984), and see 11 A.L.R. 4th 12, 81.

122. *See* pages 54–58.

123. *See*, e.g., Mechmetals Corp. v. Telex Computer Products, Inc., 709 F.2d 1287, 1293 (9th Cir. 1983), which held that a company was not entitled to shop rights in independent contractors' invention. *But see* Francklyn v. Guilford Packing Co., 695 F.2d 1158 (9th Cir. 1983), granting shop rights in an independent contractor's invention.

5. Is the worker generally excluded from fringe benefits?

"Yes" answers to these questions tend to confirm that the independent contractor or consultant label is accurate. Negative responses may support the inference that the "consultant" is really an employee.[124]

In determining whether a worker should be classified as an independent contractor or an employee, a court will generally ask whether the worker was under the employer's supervision and control, regardless of the title the worker bears.[125] For example, a photographer who took pictures of the "Royal Family" of England under a "gentleman's agreement" with Buckingham Palace was an independent contractor who held the copyright in the pictures, when the only control exercised by Buckingham Palace was arranging the sitting and a reservation of the right to review the pictures.[126]

The copyright law specifically provides for the allocation of copyright in works created by independent contractors (known as "works made for hire"). Generally, an independent contractor retains copyright in his or her creation unless there is written agreement expressly granting copyright to the hiring entity, and unless the creation falls into one of nine categories.[127] It has been held, however, that an independent contractor may be categorized as an employee for purposes of the governing statute if he or she operated under the supervision and control of the employer.[128] This theory appears to be a misconstruction of the statute, but it is unclear how future courts will decide this issue.[129]

Federal employees   A definite word of caution must be uttered concerning federal employees. These persons may be subject to various requirements regarding secrecy and ownership that are special to the federal government. The best advice for a federal employee or his attorney is to be sure to examine applicable regulations before attempting to apply the other legal principles set forth in this book. Perhaps certain persons working for state or local governments

---

124. References regarding the employer-independent contractor distinction are 51 A.L.R. Fed. 702 (1981), 55 A.L.R. Fed. 20 (1981) and Restatement (Second) of Agency, Sections 2, 220, and 229 (1958).

125. Q-Co Industries, Inc. v. Hoffman, 625 F. Supp. 608 (D.C.N.Y. 1985).

126. Sygma Photo News, Inc. v. Globe Intern., Inc., 616 F. Supp. 1153 (D.C.N.Y. 1985). *Compare* Peregrine v. Lauren Corp., 601 F. Supp. 828 (D. Col. 1985).

127. 17 U.S.C. Section 201(a) (1985).

128. Evans Newton Inc. v. Chicago Systems Software, 793 F.2d 889 (7th Cir. 1986) and Aldon Accessories v. Spiegel, 738 F.2d 548 (2d Cir.), cert. denied, 469 U.S. 982, 105 S. Ct. 387, 83 L. Ed. 2d 321 (1984). This doctrine was soundly criticized in Note, *The Works Made For Hire Doctrine Under the Copyright Act of 1976—A Misinterpretation: Aldon Accessories Ltd. v. Spiegel, Inc.*, 20 U.S.F. L. Rev. 649 (1986).

129. *See* Note, *supra.*

will be subject to special regulations in certain situations also. Bearing in mind the need to check government regulations, the following general observations can be made.

In *Kaplan v. Corcoran* (545 F.2d 1073 [7th Cir., 1976]), the court determined that the President had the authority to establish special regulations determining the ownership of inventions developed in relation to federal government employment. The rule involved, Executive Order 10096, "provides in substance that the United States shall obtain title to any invention made by any Government employee during working hours, or with a contribution by the Government, or which bears a direct relation to, or is made in consequence of, the inventor's official duties."[130] This rule, which is still in force, allows the United States government to go substantially beyond the Shop Right Doctrine and claim actual title to intellectual property itself.[131] Under circumstances in which the government's contribution to an employee's invention is "insufficient equitable to justify" an assignment of the entire right to the invention, the rule provides for reservation of a shop right in the government.[132]

U.S. government claims concerning intellectual work products were given a broad sweep and were enhanced by a postemployment covenant in *Snepp v. United States* (444 U.S. 507 [1980]). The *Snepp* case involved a book, *Decent Interval*, which had been written by Frank Snepp, a former CIA agent. The government sued Snepp claiming that he had violated a postemployment covenant in his agreement with the CIA which obliged him "not to publish or participate in the publication of any information or material relating to the Agency, its activities or intelligence activities generally, either during or after the term of my employment . . . ."[133] Based upon the contract and on Snepp's position which the court determined involved an extremely high degree of trust, the court granted the government a constructive trust over all the book profits and enjoined further violation of the agreement. Despite the *Snepp* ruling, government employees should retain substantial protections of their work product. These protections should include "the right to litigate the ownership of the information, the right to fair appor-

---

130. 37 C.F.R. 100.6 (1983) and Kaplan v. Corcoran, 545 F.2d 1073, 1074 (7th Cir., 1976). *See* Tresanky, *Patent Rights in Federal Employee Inventions*, 67 J. PAT. AND TRADEMARK OFF. 451 (1985).

131. The specific result of the case is thus contrary to that in United States v. Dubilier Condenser Corp., 289 U.S. 178 (1933) discussed on pages 49–50. The basic interpretation of shop rights and implied assignments in *Dubilier* are *not* undermined, however. The new special rule regarding federal employees was simply not in existence at the time *Dubilier* was decided. *See* 545 F.2d 1073, 1076 (7th Cir., 1976).

132. Executive Order 10096(b) (15 Fed. Reg. 389 [1950]).

133. United States v. Snepp, 595 F.2d 926, 930 (4th Cir., 1979).

tionment of profits, and the right to obtain modifications of unreasonable post-employment restraints."[134] The substance of Executive Order 10096 has been criticized as confusing and possibly unconstitutional, and legislation is urged to clarify the rights of federal employees in their work product.[135]

Finally it should be noted that if a private party is working on a United States government-sponsored project, the intellectual property claims of that party and its employees may be altered by provisions in the government contract that covers the work.[136]

Conclusion   When intellectual work products are created within an employment relationship, their ownership is determined by that relationship. The terms of the employment contract may determine property claims. These terms, however, will be conditioned and restricted by statutes and essential public policies. The employer and employee owe each other the reciprocal obligation of good faith. The nature of the specific job assignment tends to indicate which party owns resulting intellectual property. For example, a specific job assignment to invent tends to imply assignment of the ownership of the work product to the employer.

The total picture of competing intellectual property claims may be complex. Even so, it is likely that the resolution of the claims will tend to follow the five major guidelines set out in this chapter. To a large extent, these guidelines and the various rules of law will be interpreted in a common-sense way when applied to a given case. If it seems clear that the employee has taken a process which the employer kept secret, the employer will likely win the dispute. If the employer has tried to tie up the employee with a contract that ignores the employee's need to be able to move about, the employer's claim will likely fail. These kinds of results based on the guidelines are predictable. Overall they tend toward one final observation: the employee and employer are most likely to serve their own interests if they treat each other fairly and recognize each other's important interests.

---

134. H. Anawalt, *A Critical Appraisal of Snepp v. United States*, 21 Santa Clara L. Rev. 697, 726 (1981).

135. *See* Tresanky, *Patent Rights in Federal Employee Inventions*, 67 J. Pat. and Trademark Off. 451 (1985) and cases cited therein.

136. 35 U.S.C. Section 202 was recently amended to provide that when something is co-invented by a government employee and a contractor which qualifies as a non-profit organization or a small business, the federal agency involved may transfer its rights in the invention to the contractor.

CHAPTER 4

Practical Applications of the Legal Rules

A little more than a century ago, Thomas M. Cooley set about writing *A Treatise on the Law of Torts*. He hoped to set out "with reasonable clearness the general principles under which tangible and intangible rights may be claimed and their disturbance remedied in the law."[1] Early in his book he made an observation appropriate to both his time and ours.

> In a primitive state of society, while occupations are few and the transactions of business and trade are simple, the judge is seldom called upon to give redress, except for lawless and reckless conduct, where only the facts are in dispute. In the more advanced society his attention is invited to invasions of copyrights and patents, to frauds accomplished by new and peculiar methods, to questions in the law of common carriers, which are intimately connected with the new improvements in methods of transportation, and to a variety of wrongs that are new, because the conditions from which they spring, or which give occasion for them, are new. Intellectual and material progress in various ways begets a complexity of business and social relations, and this adds perpetually to the difficulties of legal administration, and multiplies with no little rapidity the occasions for an adjudication upon disputed or doubtful rights. And it renders necessary an infinity of legislation in order to adjust and harmonize the new conditions with what remains of the old.[2]

We have canvassed the rules of intellectual property and the principles of the employment relation. A number of these rules reach back to Cooley's time. Yet, as he observed, these rules have been adjusted or supplanted in an effort to "harmonize the new conditions with what remains of the old."

The rules which have been examined in the first three chapters demonstrate that intellectual property claims are determined by a process of identifying the type of ownership claim (patent, etc.) and tracing its origin through the creative work done in the employment relationship. Now we will examine certain practical consequences and applications of the rules.

---

1. THOMAS M. COOLEY, A TREATISE ON THE LAW OF TORTS OR THE WRONGS WHICH ARISE INDEPENDENT OF CONTRACT, (1879) Preface.
2. *Id.*, page 2.

It is important to remember that the rules themselves will continue to be subject to change to take account of new social and technical conditions.

Starting a new job—the employee perspective

Employee freedom and job assignments

In theory, an employment relationship begins with the negotiation of a contract.[3] In practice, it is a matter of "getting a job." With few exceptions, the employer has the leverage at the time employment commences and, predictably, will try to maximize its contract claims to idea rights at that time. The prospective employee who has little leverage or bargaining power, who must accept a job offer or go on looking, still has valuable options to exercise. If he or she expects to be using his or her inventiveness on or off the job it may be possible to have a clause written into the contract which either acknowledges a certain area of employee freedom or accords the employee substantial compensation for an invention. This option should not be overlooked. If such a provision becomes a real possibility, it is wise for the employee to have his own counsel look over the language of the proposed contract.

If the prospective employer is not willing to provide for some employee ownership in the contract, discussion may nevertheless prove useful to the employee. The employee's job assignment may be shown to have a certain scope, and this may be clarified at the outset. For example, it may be proposed that Ms. Ames be hired as a programmer for X. It becomes clear that her assignment includes the development of software related to accounting systems marketed by X. If, on her own time and effort, she develops an educational program divorced from accounting, she should be in a good position to claim that it is hers, not her employer's. This is particularly true if the limitations of the job assignment have been discussed at the outset. The employment contract should be interpreted to have reasonable scope, and the job assignment appears not to include educational software. If there is a dispute as to ownership of the educational software, the employee has improved her claim by the effort at forthright discussion at the outset. She has tried to establish reasonable limits and avoid "a mortgage on her brain."[4] The exact outcome of any such dispute will depend on the employment contract, its reasonableness, her job assignment, the consistency of the employer's behavior, and the way that the parties have interpreted their obligations by their actions.[5]

---

3. Please *see* pages 35–36.
4. *See* pages 54–58.
5. Please *see* pages 35–37 and 54–58.

The employer point of view

From the company point of view, the educational software example given on the previous pages is troubling. Let us suppose that the employer has a very strong idea and invention assignment provision in the contract. The employment contract might provide, for example:

1. I hereby assign and agree to assign to X Corporation my entire right, title, and interest in any invention, trade secret, work of authorship, proprietary information, or proprietary thing or idea hereafter made or conceived solely by me or jointly with others . . . which relates to any actual or anticipated business, research, development, product, service, or activity of X Corporation.
2. I will disclose promptly in writing any such invention or other item covered by Section 1 upon creation, conception, or by otherwise becoming aware of it.[6]

X Company's activities include the production and marketing of certain educational materials, namely books. These are handled by a different division than the one Ms. Ames works for.[7]

A manager for X Corporation, having read the remarks regarding Ms. Ames and her educational program says, "You mean to say that Ms. Ames may own an educational program she wrote while working for us? In spite of her contract?" The answer is "Yes!" The company may reach too far with its effort to preempt each and every thing she might create. If she writes a poem or a short story at home, certainly one would argue that the company should not own that. The educational program is removed from her work also. Assuming that she has been loyal and effective in her job, it is reasonable to interpret the scope of her contract with X as requiring assignment of those works of authorship which relate to her work assignment and which are produced with company time or resources.

The company's true interests are probably job related. It wants her effort, loyalty, and ingenuity applied to the work she does for the company. Of course, the company does not want her to utilize her efforts to develop a competing accounting software, but it appears that the company has not established any expectation on its part or hers that she will apply herself to the development of educational programs.

From the employer's perspective, it is wise to tailor invention and idea restrictions so that they relate to the job assignment. It is also appropriate to build compensation for inventive work into the contract. This compen-

Compensation for inventiveness

---

6. Other examples of such provisions appear on pages 54–58.

7. A different division of a company is likely to be treated as a separate employer under California law. *See* pages 46–47. Therefore, the employer's claim based on its other divisions' activities should be very weak in that state.

sation should be substantial. Substantial compensation encourages inventiveness and initiative and tends to avoid objections that the contract is unreasonable. The employer should be aware that it may have to deal with a range of legal objections when it comes to enforcing an employment agreement. As we have seen, these include: unconscionability, employee mobility, adequacy of compensation, actual job assignment, vagueness, practical construction of the contract, and reasonableness.[8]

When one examines employment contract invention provisions, one notes that the aspect that usually reaches too far is the one which claims employer ownership for inventions and ideas "that relate in any manner to the actual or anticipated business, research, development, product, services, or activities . . . of X Corporation." This type of provision defies employee interest in personal mobility and reasonable self-interest. A creative and dedicated programmer may be able to produce all that is related to her job and still develop a sideline outside the company. These outside activities need not detract from her work nor involve the taking of company property or ideas. If she is too exhausted by her other activities or goes into direct competition, she can be admonished and disciplined. But no company owns a worker's life. Furthermore, an energetic worker is going to do something else other than work anyway—run marathons, play an instrument, write, or enjoy night life. The employer should be pleased if some of that activity is related to the employee's calling. Usually this extra activity rewards the employer anyway. It is not necessary to try to tie up the employee with contract clauses that are greedy.

The prospective employee who has leverage

Bargaining from ability

The prospective employee who has a proven background or inventive ability presents a special case both for himself and for the prospective employer. First of all, he or she should become aware of his or her value in this regard. This allows him to approach the bargaining process realistically.

Second, this type of employee should bargain clearly and effectively to serve his reasonable self interests. If fact, there will be little room for the new employee "with clout" to complain about unconscionability or the unreasonable scope of invention provisions if he has had the opportunity to bargain at the outset and has not exercised it. Usually the employer will not simply offer a "take it or leave it" proposition to such a person. The

---

8. Related discussions are presented in chapter 3, particularly those sections on unconscionability (pages 38–39), mobility (pages 42–43), adequacy (pages 43–44), job assignment (pages 52–53), and pages 62–65.

person who simply goes ahead and accepts a restrictive covenant under such conditions has not been forced or pressured, and it is appropriate to argue that the employee himself has interpreted the restrictions as reasonable.

The talented employee will often best be served by consulting an attorney or other advisor before entering into the employment relationship. This is one way to protect one's expectations. The experience of professional athletes and entertainers indicates that the use of an advisor may be an important ingredient in successful bargaining. Consultation with an attorney need not be elaborate and the attorney need not be brought directly into the process. You may simply arrange for a consultation with the lawyer to see what the evaluation of the proposed contract is, and you can proceed with the direct negotiation yourself.

In most respects the employer is able to deal with a prospect who has leverage in the same way as with other new employees. In some ways, the employer's position is even a bit more secure when it establishes relationships with such an employee. The company knows, or should be aware, that there is more equality in the bargaining process. It should be willing to be realistic in terms of compensation and invention limitations. Failure in this regard is more likely to be self-correcting at the outset—the talented employee may go elsewhere or terminate employment prematurely. Also, if a "hard bargain" is struck, the employer is less likely to be shown to have acted unconscionably.

Developing a sideline

One theme of this book is that the employee has certain rights to develop a sideline or additional inventive activity outside his or her employment. This is based on an assessment of the legal principles and decided cases that have been reviewed. It is not an unlimited right, but it is an option which remains open to an employee and which enjoys certain definite legal protections.

There are certain rules of thumb which an employee can observe to enhance his or her protection in developing a sideline.

Don't poach on your employer's terrain. Do not try to use your employer's specific plans or projects for your outside advantage. This is a corollary of the general rule that one must not appropriate things that belong to the employer. (See Guideline 5 on page 59.) The lines are not easy to draw, and in some cases the employee will, in fact, be justified in coming very close to the employer's line of work or ideas in his sideline developments. In general, however, it is best to develop a sideline that uses your skills in a different specific application than that of your employer.

Rules for sideline protection

Do not use your employer's time, equipment, or supplies in your sideline. Some incidental use should not result in forfeiture of idea work that is your own, but if there is a pattern of using your employer's materials, etc., then you are much less justified in your claim to independent work product. Although a very minimal use probably will not result in the loss of ownership, any use could be subject to scrutiny by the court. Therefore, the best rule is to steer clear of such use.[9]

Make necessary disclosures.   If you begin an outside activity, there will come some point when you should probably disclose that fact to your employer. That point may be reached at the outset of other activity, or it may occur later on. If there is little tendency toward conflict between your outside activity and your employment, then later or more casual disclosure may be sufficient.

If you begin to develop an idea of potential interest to your employer, however, the point of decision regarding disclosure has certainly arrived. The advantages of disclosure are that you will have given your employer a chance to act and you will fulfill disclosure obligations under a contract. (See, for example, the contract provision discussed on page 75.) The disadvantages are that your employer may seek to interfere with your activities or be alerted to make intellectual property claims that you believe are unwarranted or unfair. One compromise is to give a strictly limited disclosure. For example, Ms. Ames might disclose that "I have been working with a group of friends, and we are well on the way toward the development of a piece of educational software." Failure of the employer to pursue the matter after notice will tend to show no interest on its part and strengthen your claims to absolute ownership. On the other hand, an immediate demand that you assign your rights or that you stop your activities will alert you that the employer (or your immediate boss) may be taking a heavyhanded approach and that you should look into some appropriate countermeasures.

Disclosure is a good general rule, but it is an approach which requires a certain finesse and may not always be justified.

A case example will illustrate the delicacy of deciding whether to disclose, and if so, how much to disclose. In *Science Accessories Corporation v. Sumagraphics Corporation* (425 A.2d 957 [Del. 1984]), former key development and engineering employees were sued by Science Accessories (SAC) because they had allegedly set up a competing corporation and diverted a corporate opportunity to it while they were still employed by SAC. SAC was in the business of developing and marketing computer graphics equipment. A non-employee, Dr. Alfred Brenner, had developed a val-

---

9. *See, e.g.,* Banner Metals v. Lockwood, 178 Cal. App. 2d 643, 3 Cal. Rptr. 198 (1962).

uable new type of "mag wire digitizer" for use in the computer graphics process.[10] SAC claimed that while serving as employees, the defendants had "learned of Brenner's mag wire concept, secreted the information from SAC, converted the concept into a 'bread board' or working model, and then diverted the concept from SAC to Sumagraphics in breach of their duties to SAC, both fiduciary and contractual."[11] In support of its case, SAC could rely on a strong employee invention and disclosure agreement signed by the employees. (The language of the agreement was virtually identical to the language of the contract set out on page 75.) Nonetheless, the trial court denied SAC any relief, and the Delaware Supreme Court affirmed.

SAC had no right to nonemployee Brenner's ideas or inventions, but it arguably had a very good claim to the key employees' actual use of such an idea during the term of employment. The Delaware Supreme Court agreed that the employees had a duty of loyalty, but it noted that they were nevertheless "free to make reasonable preparations to compete while still employed by SAC." The concealment of plans to enter competition where they had used their own time and resources to develop a product "was not, without more, a violation of their fiduciary duty of loyalty." The court noted that to require employees to divulge such information to their employers "would create an undesirable impediment to free competition in the commercial and industrial sectors of our economy."[12]

A Maryland court has also commented on the area of employee loyalty and disclosure. In *Maryland Metals, Inc. v. Metzner* (282 Md. 31, 382 A.2d 564 [1978]), a corporate vice president, Metzner, and another employee were sued by their former employer for having made plans to enter into competition with it while they were still employees. The company claimed that Metzner and the other employee were obliged to disclose in detail their preliminary arrangements to go into competition with Maryland Metals. The court disagreed. The court stated that "a corporate officer or employee owes undivided and unselfish loyalty to the corporation." This obliges an employee to be candid with the employer, but does not oblige the employee to reveal the precise nature of his plans "unless he has acted inimically to the employer's interests beyond the mere failure to disclose."[13] It is important to remember that statutes in many states reflect a strong policy against placing restraints on one's ability to practice a trade.[14]

Segregate your activity.   This is implied in the first rule of thumb dealing with poaching on the employer's terrain. Keep your sideline activity

---

10. 425 A.2d 957, 960–961.
11. *Id.* at 961.
12. *Id.* at 965.
13. 282 Md. 31, 382 A.2d 564, 569 (1978).
14. *See, e.g.,* Cal. Bus. & Prof. Code Section 16600.

and your job separate from each other. Use your own supplies and time. You may join with fellow employees in the sideline; in fact that was the situation in both the *Science Accessories* and *Metzner* cases. If you do join with others, however, you must be doubly careful, because there will be a greater risk of utilizing the employer's ideas or poaching on his time. As the *Metzner* case emphasized, the privilege to go ahead and prepare to compete does not immunize employees from liability for misconduct, including misappropriation of trade secrets, misuse of confidential information, solicitation of customers, conspiracy to bring about a mass resignation, or usurpation of employer business opportunities.

Keep up with your employer's work. You have a job. Do it. Give it all of its deserved attention. Or quit!

Get legal protection of your products as they come into being. You should obtain patent, copyright, trademark, and trade secret protections as these become appropriate. (See Chapter 2.)

Good faith. Treat your employer and its business with good faith. It cannot be overemphasized how important good faith is on both sides of the employment relationship. This means to be fair. We can catalog some of the elements of fairness. The rules of thumb on poaching, disclosure, segregation of activity, and honest effort are examples. In addition, there are others. There are situations that you know "don't sit well." Obey the sense. Talk over the problem with someone you trust. If he or she agrees that something sounds wrong with what you propose to do, the chances are that something is.

The employer's view of outside activities

Justifiable expectations   The employer has a justifiable expectation that the employee will observe the six rules of thumb which are set out in the previous section. That is, the employer may expect that its employees will:

1. Not poach on the employer's interest;
2. Give reasonable disclosures of outside activities, especially those which might conflict with employer business;
3. Segregate work and outside activities;
4. Devote full energy to assigned work;
5. Protect employer intellectual property; and
6. Act in good faith.

Employers need to be reminded that they may bear a particularly heavy burden when it comes to protecting trade secrets. Any valuable process may be a trade secret if it is kept secret. (See pages 23–24.) The important thing is to identify secret processes and maintain the secrecy. (See pages 25–28.)

The employer can act to protect its interests by creating reasonable policies and rules governing employee conduct. These should be communicated to the employees. The employer should inquire about outside activities, when this seems appropriate. It should continue to identify truly secret items. Overly broad or unnecessarily restrictive employee rules or guidelines should be eliminated. Such rules are likely to be disregarded by courts. Overly restrictive rules are likely to be viewed as "little more than attempts to intimidate or threaten employees" or as an interference with legitimate job mobility.[15]

Rules for employee conduct

A healthy job relationship

It is best to cultivate a healthy relationship between employer and employee. The employment relationship is a contract, and one should avoid entering into a contract where one feels that he or she cannot really cooperate with the other party. One should enter a contract hoping to accomplish the agreed objectives. When rancor or suspicion creeps into the relationship, the objectives of the contract tend to be frustrated. This is especially true with respect to employment relationships.

A contract is supposed to allow parties to set their own rules of behavior. If they do not cooperate with each other, however, the rules may end up being ignored.

The employment relationship differs from many contracts in that employees are usually not as free to make choices as contract theory assumes. Economic pressures and limited opportunity often dictate the range of choices which are open to the employee, and too often this range is small. Normally the employer has much more range or choice. Consequently, the onus of achieving cooperation lies largely with the employer and its management. On the other hand, the employee should do his or her full part to make the relationship work.

Employer/employee conflicts over invention rights pose a distinct threat to a healthy job relationship. The employer can reduce these tensions by offering strong incentives or compensation for useful employee innovations. The employee can reduce these tensions by offering his or her inventions to the employer when it is felt that this choice is justified.[16]

---

15. The quotation in the text comes from the Minnesota Supreme Court's discussion of sloppy trade secret practices in Electrocraft Corporation v. Controlled Motion, Inc., 332 N.W. 2d 890, 903 (Minn. 1983) which is discussed on pages 60–61.

16. Sometimes an employee is legally bound to offer his invention to an employer, while at other times he or she is not. See pages 54–58.

If a suspicious or unfriendly relationship develops, it should be remedied. If such a relationship continues, perhaps both the employer and the employee should explore their other options, including dissolving the relationship.

Changing jobs

If employee inventiveness leads to a job change or employee efforts to set up a separate business, both the employer and the employee will be concerned with the following items:

1. Each party should review the existing employment contract. See pages 35–38 and Guideline Number 1 in chapter 3.
2. The employer and the employee should each remind themselves of the essential interests of the other party. Please review Guideline Number 3 on page 47.
3. Each party should review the implications of the current job assignment. In this regard, please see pages 52–58, and Guideline Number 4 in chapter 3 on page 53.
4. The employee must be very careful not to appropriate any of the employer's trade secrets or other property. There can be some very close judgment calls in this area. In general, the employer has an obligation to be reasonably clear in preserving secrecy. If the employer has not been clear in identifying those items which are secret or which should be preserved, then the employee may have a legitimate argument that no trade secret was taken. See pages 58–62 and Guideline Number 5. The employee should remember, however, that in no event is he or she free to appropriate the employer's patents or copyrights.
5. The departing employee should make necessary disclosures. On the other hand, the employer should seek the appropriate disclosures of information from its employees. See pages 78–79.
6. Both parties should get necessary legal advice.
7. Both parties should use common sense and make every effort to be fair. Please see pages 35–37 and 77–80.

Going to court

Litigation over invention ownership is expensive, and it also consumes time and mental energy. Most individuals who become involved in litigation "live the lawsuit." Resorting to the courts is, nevertheless, sometimes necessary. If it appears necessary to go to court, the following observations are helpful to the parties and their counsel.

Early advice.   Usually it is advisable to get an early legal opinion on whether and how to proceed once it becomes clear that litigation is a real possibility. In an employer/employee contest the employer will usually be in a position to seek this advice from its regular counsel. The employee may have to find an attorney, but should not delay doing so.

Negotiations continue.   The choice to litigate does not foreclose the possibility of negotiation or even amicable resolution of the dispute. Negotiations should continue. Once a lawsuit commences, each party should consult with its own attorney concerning appropriate overtures or positions in negotiation. Ordinarily, negotiations are conducted by the attorneys once a lawsuit commences, but it is my opinion that the parties should continue to consider face-to-face attempts to resolve a problem. If you wish to have a face-to-face negotiation, simply discuss this with your attorney.

Temporary restraining orders and injunctions.   Usually intellectual property claims include a request for a court order such as an injunction to stop using a process. When this is the case, the very first order, such as a temporary restraining order (TRO), is often the most critical. Assume that a former employee has formed a company, and that the new company's work will be based on a certain critical process. The former employer may go to court and obtain a temporary restraining order preventing the use of that process. The TRO may have the effect of stopping production and placing a cloud over business relations for the new company. Lawyers for high technology businesses are generally well aware of the effect of the first order and use its leverage accordingly.

"Big guys" versus "little guys."   In a court battle the larger economic entity usually enjoys a large advantage. It can more likely afford the expense and uncertainty of legal action. It is often able to make a much larger outlay for attorneys' services and procedures. By contrast, the small economic entity, usually the former employee, will feel the expense and the stress more quickly and more personally. He or she is likely to feel overwhelmed by a barrage of paper and procedure.

Getting a lawyer

Obtaining a lawyer is a critical step in evaluating a contract, in determining whether one has an intellectual property right, and in preparing for appropriate actions in court. Generally, larger employers have legal departments or established attorney support systems. The small employer or the individual employee may be in the position of needing to choose a lawyer to fit a particular occasion. If a lawyer has previously helped with some matter, say the filing of articles of incorporation or the writing of a will, that person may or may not be the appropriate person to handle your new inquiry.

In selecting a lawyer you should ask questions concerning the attorney's knowledge and background. Prior experience with intellectual property questions is a plus factor, but such things as a good negotiating style and trial experience are positive attributes, too. You might even ask if the lawyer feels qualified in the area and why he or she thinks so. Do not neglect to ask about fees. This is an entirely appropriate thing to discuss.

See more than one lawyer, if you wish, before you decide. On some legal questions it is useful to get a second opinion. This is also entirely appropriate. It is usually best to let your first lawyer know that you wish to seek such a second opinion. After all, lawyers wish to be treated with general respect and courtesy as much as any other individuals.

In the end it is up to you to decide who your lawyer will be. It is my opinion that many lawyers can qualify themselves to handle the problems which have been presented in this book (however, please recall that only patent lawyers are permitted to process a patent application. Please see page 9). It is essential, however, that the lawyer dig deeply into intellectual property and employment law if he or she is to be effective. The facts of the case must be thoroughly understood and assessed. Choosing a lawyer is much like choosing a work environment or a job. You should satisfy yourself on two essential questions. Does this person appear qualified? Will I be able to work with him or her? If these are answered affirmatively, you have a good basis for a lawyer-client relationship.

CHAPTER 5

Planning

The need for a plan

In some cases it may be rather easy to resolve competing claims of ownership of idea products. For example, the matter may be covered by a clear contract provision which is apparently very reasonable. Not all disputes, however, will be resolved by simple reference to a contract or employee handbook. Instead, the provisions of the contract or handbook may be taken into account along with facts concerning the relative contribution of effort, origin of the idea, reasonableness of the contract provisions, and good faith performance.

There is a certain flexibility in the rules which govern the ownership of idea products which are developed during employment. The flexibility is intended to achieve equitable results between the parties, but it also has the effect of making ownership claims more uncertain. The element of uncertainty is compounded by the delay and expense which are encountered in the formal legal system. In addition, Americans have become increasingly willing, or even eager, to resort to the courts either to resolve disagreements, or to set the stage for their resolution.

The combined factors of uncertainty, delay, expense, and litigiousness create a very unsettling picture. No wonder people in business want to avoid entanglement in legal controversy. However, a technology-oriented business is likely to have some kind of conflict over ownership rights, and one cannot simply wish these problems away. It is better to be prepared in advance. Both the employer and the employee need a plan which will take into account the legal rules of ownership.

Use legal advice

Probably all employers in fields involving intellectual property need to include the legal concepts which we have discussed in their business plans. The same thing is true for individual employees who wish to develop some extracurricular use of their ideas.

Legal awareness is important in planning, but one should avoid becoming legalistic in one's approach to business. Certain basic legal guidelines need to be at the forefront of any person's attention in business. These include awareness of the need to avoid fraud, misrepresentation, discrimination, bribery, and so forth. These basics also include such concepts as the obligation to apply a good faith effort in the performance of any job or contract. These legal "rules" have emerged from common, human expectations. Thus, they can be followed without diverting one's attention from the work at hand. They are like the rules of a sport—one does not expect to be permitted to play offside in soccer or to score a point on an "out" shot in tennis.

However, most of us have encountered people who conduct their business as if they had only an eye for legal consequences. Some business people use the law as a kind of offense, trying to drive the hardest legal bargain. Some professionals worry too much about defending themselves from legal claims. Certain doctors and lawyers take some actions only because they "don't want to be sued." In these instances, legal considerations seem to have obscured the fundamental enterprise—to accomplish the productive purpose of a business, or to render appropriate professional services.

There are three steps which may be taken which will allow one to include legal considerations in an effective plan without falling into these extremes. First, one needs to become aware of legal demands which relate especially to one's occupation. In the present case, if you are an employer or employee in the idea product field, you need to know:

1. Generally what patent, copyright, and trade secrets are.
2. The five guidelines of Chapter 3—the importance of the employment contract, the role of good faith, the utility of respecting essential interests, the impact of job assignments, and respect for employer property.

Once the general ideas have been reviewed and understood, you will be able to act with poise and tact regarding the development process and its potential for conflict over valuable property rights.

The second ingredient is outside advice—usually that of a lawyer. A lawyer's job is to develop a good legal plan for you. To do this, the lawyer must be "legalistic" in the sense that he or she must attend to legal details. At the same time, good legal advice is built on reminding the client of the larger picture. The second ingredient in a plan is getting effective legal answers during the planning phase. Do not wait. Legal advice, when needed, becomes more expensive when you procrastinate. The second step involves consulting with an advisor and making decisions on how to incorporate certain legal protections into an overall plan.

The third step is to build certain review mechanisms into your plan. This can be done by reviewing certain checklists, such as the ones set out in the next two sections.

An employer checklist

The following checklist highlights employer concerns with work products developed in the context of employment. It should be used in connection with overall business planning, including elements which are beyond strictly legal concerns.

Employer concerns with work products

1. Determine which jobs have responsibilities that include design, invention, or creativity.
2. Determine which of these jobs should be covered by invention assignment, invention disclosure, and noncompetition clauses of a contract.
3. Draft appropriate and reasonable contract provisions. Usually an attorney should review these.
4. Present the invention provisions to the employee. This should be done at the commencement of employment, if possible.
5. Explain the provisions and discuss them with the employee.
6. Watch for employee resistance to the provisions. Employee uneasiness may indicate that the provisions are counterproductive.
7. Review contracts periodically. Are they reasonable?
8. Consider providing substantial incentives or compensation for employee invention.
9. Keep informed about employees' activities. Distinguish between genuine conflict of interest and activities which are not threatening.
10. Avoid being intrusive, however. Be respectful of employee privacy and freedom of activity.
11. Keep employees informed of what items are truly secret.
12. Establish reasonable in-house guidelines on who should receive what information. (See also pages 26–28.)
13. Consider adopting an employee manual. If a manual is appropriate for your business, it should contain informative, clear, and reasonable guidelines.
14. Clearly outline plans or expectations with regard to particular project assignments involving design, invention, or creativity when discussing these with employees assigned to the project.
15. Consider adopting an active invention review system so you can identify ideas which may be patented, copyrighted, or utilized in the business, and act quickly regarding application or registration.
16. When an employee invents something or develops an outside activity, review the employee activities to determine your inven-

tion rights. Do not delay. If an employee approaches you with an invention, accept or reject it as promptly as possible.

17. Consider interviewing or discussing matters with an inventive employee who appears ready to leave employment.

18. When an employee leaves employment, conduct an appropriate exit interview. The employee should be reminded of his or her obligations and be given specific guidance on items which must be kept confidential.

Employee checklists

The following checklists deal with the employee's interests in protecting his or her idea products. These checklists are divided into three related categories: a checklist related to the commencement of employment; a checklist dealing with one's job and one's outside activities; and finally a checklist dealing with changing jobs.

Commencing employment

1. Define your job expectations and goals.
2. If invention, creativity or self-employment is a realistic goal, take this into account in your employment search.
3. Study closely any written employment contract which is offered to you.
4. Review the following employment contract provisions carefully: the invention disclosure provisions, the invention assignment provisions, and noncompetition clauses.
5. Clarify your job assignment and job responsibilities with your prospective employer.
6. Consider creating a written statement of your job assignment either in the employment contract or in a confirming memorandum.
7. Consider requesting a provision that specifically recognizes your invention rights and/or provides for specific compensation for your invention rights. It may be difficult to obtain a provision which recognizes substantial rights.
8. Consult a lawyer or other advisor on important questions such as the meaning of the invention assignment provisions, requirements of disclosure, implications of job assignment, etc.

Your job and outside activities

1. Once you have become employed, give the full, deserved attention to your job.
2. Identify potential conflicts of interest between yourself and your employer.

3. Protect your employer's intellectual property.
4. If you develop a sideline activity, be sure to segregate that activity from your employer's job requirements. See pages 79–80.
5. Obtain legal advice and protection for your own idea products.
6. Make appropriate disclosures to your employer.
7. Treat your employer with good faith.

Changing jobs

1. If you plan to change jobs or to leave your employment and go into business for yourself, review all the items in the second checklist and review pages 77–80 of this book.
2. Identify all the employer's potential trade secrets or other intellectual property.
3. Obtain advice concerning what intellectual work products belong to the employer, what work products belong to you, and what items are matters of "public domain."
4. Consider appropriate timing and notice to your employer. Obtain advice on this aspect.
5. Cooperate honestly in employment termination proceedings, such as exit interviews.
6. Plan realistically for the possibility of a lawsuit against you or your new business.

Contract provisions

In preparing this book, I reviewed many different standard employment agreements. These are agreements which are prepared by employers in a standard format for signature by prospective employees or persons already employed by the company. They are often handed to the employee in a standard printed form for signature. A variation on this approach is to have an "individualized" employment agreement typed up by a word processor and submitted to the employee. I also reviewed a number of different employee manuals and other documents such as statements of understanding concerning employee restrictions. (Please see pages 65–67.)

This section sets forth three different documents which are in actual use by three large corporations. The names of the corporations have been deleted, and the companies are now called "A company," "B company," and "C company." The first document is what may be termed a rather even-handed employment agreement. The second is a somewhat stiffer, employer-dominant agreement regarding confidential information and intellectual property. The third is an "assignment of inventions agreement" by which the employer attempts to lay claim to all inventions of any kind which are made by the employee during his or her employment or within six months of termination of the employment. Each of these agreements is followed by a brief set of comments. Since I believe that the interests of both the employer and the employee are best served by an evenhanded document, it is my opinion that the first document is preferable to the second. In my view, the third document is unacceptable. I wish to add, the documents were supplied to me voluntarily by the companies concerned. I am commenting critically upon these documents, but I wish to thank these companies and others for their cooperation in supplying such information to me.[1]

---

1. The various companies which have written invention, disclosure, and non-competition agreements have been voyaging in difficult legal waters. When the company representatives write contracts, such as the examples set forth in the text, they are probably putting forth their best effort to preserve the company's interests. Now and in the future, the countervailing interests of the employee and the need for equity in employment contracts will become more apparent.

Agreement A

A Company

California
Employment Agreement
Regarding Proprietary Developments
and Confidential Information

Name: _____
(Type or Print)

I. I am a paid employee of A Company (A)

II. This Agreement concerns inventions, improvements, data, processes, computer software programs and discoveries (hereinafter called "Proprietary Developments") that are conceived or made by me alone or with others while I am employed by A; that relate to the research and development of the business of A, or result from tasks assigned to me by A; and that do not qualify fully under the provisions of California Labor Code Section 2870.* Such Proprietary Developments are the sole property of A, and I agree:

1. to disclose them promptly to A
2. to assign them to A; and
3. to execute all documents and do all things necessary to assist A in obtaining patent, copyright and/or trade secret protection in all countries, A to pay the expenses.

III. This Agreement also concerns trade secrets, confidential business and technical information, and know-how not generally known to the public, that are acquired or produced by me in connection with my employment by A. As to these, I agree:

1. to use them only in the performance of A duties; and
2. to hold them in confidence and trust, and to use all reasonable precautions to assure that they are not disclosed to unauthorized persons or used in an unauthorized manner, both during and after my employment with A.

IV. Upon termination of employment, I will not take with me any documents or materials of any nature relating to the subject matter described in paragraphs II and III above.

V. The above provisions shall be separately construed. If any of them is held to be unenforceable, the remaining provisions shall not be affected.

_____
Signature

_____
Date

Witness:

_____

*§2870. Employment agreements; assignment of rights.
Any provision in an employment agreement which provides that an employee shall assign or offer to assign any of his or her rights in an invention to his or her employer shall not apply to an invention for which no equipment, supplies, facility, or trade secret information of the employer was used and which was developed entirely on the employee's own time and (a) which does not relate (1) to the business of the employer or (2) to the employer's actual or demonstrably anticipated research or development, or (b) which does not result from any work performed by the employee for the employer. Any provision which purports to apply to such an invention is to that extent against the public policy of this state and is to that extent void and unenforceable.

June 1982

Comments on Agreement A

The first impressive feature of this agreement is that it is short, easy to read, and easy to understand. It is comprehensive in terms of its coverage of inventions, yet it restricts the company's claim to those inventions which "relate to the research and development of the business of A or result from tasks assigned to me by A." Thus the company does not appear to attempt to reach beyond developments which are within a reasonable scope of its actual interests. The company has avoided making claims to items of "potential interest" to A.[2]

Nevertheless, the agreement could be improved in the following respects in order to achieve greater objective evenhandedness: first of all, since A is a big company, the scope of A's claims to proprietary developments should be restricted to the particular division in which the employee serves. Second, the company should be prepared to administer this contract in a way which does not lay claim to employee inventions which are not related to the employee's actual job assignment. For example, A may be a company which develops certain forms of computer software. If the employee develops a computer program on his or her own time, and the program is not related to the employee's job assignment, then A company should refrain from laying claim to that program. Instead, the company should ask for a description of the program, and if it is interested in it, should offer to buy it from the employee. To do otherwise is to reach beyond the reasonable expectations of such a contract.[3]

The A company agreement neatly combines the disclosure agreement, the invention assignment agreement, and the protection of trade secret obligations. The employee is put on fair notice that he or she must disclose applicable developments promptly to A company. The employee is also reminded to "use all reasonable precautions" to care for A's trade secrets and confidential information. With respect to these items, the employer should be reminded of its need to be clear about the identification of confidential and trade secret items throughout the course of the employment relationship.[4]

---

2. *See* pages 54–58 and 74–76.
3. *See* pages 54–58, 74–76, and 77–80.
4. *See* pages 59–62.

Agreement B

B Company

Agreement Regarding Confidential Information and Intellectual Property

In consideration of my employment by B Company (B) or my continued employment at will by B, and the payment to me of the salary or other compensation that I shall receive during my employment, I agree as follows:

1. I will not, without B's prior written permission, disclose to anyone outside of B or use in other than B's business, either during or after my employment, any confidential information or material of B or its subsidiaries, or any information or material received in confidence from third parties by B or its subsidiaries. If I leave the employ of B, I will return all B property in my possession, including all confidential information or material such as drawings, notebooks, reports, and other documents.

   Confidential information or material of B or its subsidiaries is any information or material:

   (a) generated or collected by or utilized in the operations of B or its subsidiaries that relates to the actual or anticipated business or research and development of B or its subsidiaries; or

   (b) suggested by or resulting from any task assigned to me or work performed by me for or on behalf of B, and which has not been made available generally to the public.

2. I will not disclose to B, use in B's business, or cause B to use, any information or material which is confidential to others.

3. I will comply, and do all things necessary for B and its subsidiaries to comply, with the laws and regulations of all governments under which B does business, and with provisions of contracts between any such government or its contractors and B or its subsidiaries that relate to intellectual property or to the safeguarding of information.

4. I hereby assign to B my entire right, title and interest in any idea, invention, design of a useful article (whether the design is ornamental or otherwise), computer program and related documentation, and other work of authorship (all hereinafter called "Developments"), hereafter made or conceived solely or jointly by me, or written wholly or in part by me, whether or not such Developments are patentable, copyrightable or susceptible to other forms of protection, and the Developments:

   (a) relate to the actual or anticipated business or research or development of B or its subsidiaries; or

   (b) are suggested by or result from any task assigned to me or work performed by me for or on behalf or B.

   In the case of any "other work of authorship," such assignment shall be limited to those works of authorship which meet both conditions (a) and (b) above.

   The above provisions concerning assignment of Developments apply only while I am employed by B in an executive, managerial, product or technical planning, technical, research, programming or engineering capacity (including development, product, manufacturing, systems, applied science, and field engineering). Excluded are any Developments that I cannot assign to B because of prior agreement with

   _____ which is effective until

   _____ *(Give name and date or write "none").*

   I acknowledge that the copyright and any other intellectual property right in designs, computer programs and related documentation, and works of authorship, created within the scope of my employment, belong to B by operation of law.

5. In connection with any of the Developments assigned by Paragraph 4:

    (a) I will promptly disclose them to B Patent Operations or B management as appropriate; and

    (b) I will, on B's request, promptly execute a specific assignment of title to B and do anything else reasonably necessary to enable B to secure a patent, copyright or other form of protection therefor in the United States and in other countries.

6. B and its subsidiaries and their licensees (direct and indirect) are not required to designate me as author of any design, computer program or related documentation, or other work of authorship assigned in Paragraph 4 when distributed publicly or otherwise, not to make any distribution. I waive and release, to the extent permitted by law, all my rights to the foregoing.

7. I have identified on the back hereof all Developments not assigned by Paragraph 4 in which I have any right, title or interest, and which were previously made or conceived solely or jointly by me, or written wholly or in part by me, but neither published nor filed in any patent office.

    If I do not have any to identify, I have written "none" on this line:_____

    (It is in your interest to establish that any of the above were made, conceived or written before your employment by B. You should not disclose them in detail, but identify them only by the titles and dates of documents describing them. If you wish to interest B in any of them, you may contact External Submissions at Corporate Headquarters, which will provide you with instructions for submitting them to B.)

8. The term "subsidiaries," as used in this Agreement, includes any entity owned or controlled, directly or indirectly, by B.

9. With respect to the subject matter hereof, this is my entire agreement with B, and it supersedes (to the extent enforceable) all previous oral or written communications, representations, understandings, undertakings, or agreements by or with B.

10. I acknowledge receipt of a copy of this Agreement.

Signed:_____ Employee's Serial:_____ Date: _____
    Employee's Full Name

B Representative: _____   Date: _____
        Employee's Manager or other
        appropriate Representative

(If you have entered "none" in Paragraph 7, do not fill in this section.)

The following are Developments not covered by Paragraph 4, in which I have any right, title or interest, and which were previously conceived or written either wholly or in part by me, but neither published nor filed in any Patent Office:

Description of Documents (if applicable):

Title on Document	Date on Document	Name of Witness on Document
_____	_____	_____
_____	_____	_____
_____	_____	_____
_____	_____	_____

Signed: _____
        Employee's Full Name

Date: _____

This agreement is "stiffer," or more employer-dominant, than Agreement A. It is objectionable because it attempts to reach "the actual or anticipated business or research or development" of B or any of its subsidiaries. This claim sweeps beyond the reasonable expectations of the job relationship.[5]

B company assignment provisions would undoubtedly be invalid in California. Under California law, B has a right to claim inventions only if these relate to the employer's "actual or demonstrably anticipated research or development" or which results from some work performed by the employee for the employer.[6] B company's agreement also goes beyond the permissible bounds of California law by requiring the assignment of invention rights which may be related to interests of a subsidiary of B corporation. The B company agreement contains a useful provision which is not present in the A company agreement. This is item 2, which reminds the employee of an obligation not to take advantage of some other person's trade secrets or confidential information. (It must be emphasized, however, that this is simply a useful reminder. If B company is to guard itself against appropriation of the work of others, it must take reasonable day-to-day precautions in that regard. It cannot protect itself simply by putting a reminder of an obligation into an employee's contract.)

Alternatives which are available to B company include: drafting a more limited provision, as is the case in the agreement established by company A; and establishing a realistic employee compensation provision. There should be quite a variety of possibilities concerning realistic employee compensation schemes. For example, the employer might establish a standard royalty percentage which bears a reasonable relationship to royalties which independent inventors might obtain through a bargained assignment of their invention. This figure might be discounted in favor of the employer in order to reflect the fact that the inventing employee has had the job security and employment opportunity to sustain him or her during the invention process. Another option might be to establish some kind of an invention assignment board which would make offers to the inventing employee. Still another possibility is to grant the inventing employee a fixed percentage royalty, and to provide that another fixed percentage should go into a fund which is designed to benefit all employees of the company. Such a fund might be earmarked for such items as the education of employees or their dependents. The purpose of this latter type of provision would be to preserve employee morale throughout the company. In this way, all of the employees would feel that they are the beneficiaries of the inventions which are made by their colleagues. This would tend to counterbalance a feeling that only "superstars" are rewarded.

Comments on Agreement B

---

5. *See* pages 43–47, 54–58, 74–76, and 77–80.
6. *See* page 43.

The B company agreement also reaches too far in the area of required nondisclosures. There is a recognized interest on the part of any company to protect its trade secrets and confidential information, but to insist that this confidential information includes any information which is "suggested by or resulting from any task assigned" to the employee invades the individual's realm of personal autonomy. It is not reasonable to insist that B company's interests reach that far.

Agreement C

C Company

Assignment of Inventions Agreement

I, the undersigned, as a condition precedent to my employment by the Corporation, and as part consideration for wages or salary paid to me in the event of such employment, hereby agree as follows:

1. "Corporation"—The term "Corporation" as used herein means C Corporation and all divisions and subsidiaries thereof.

2. "Inventions"—The term "Inventions" as used herein means all ideas, inventions, discoveries and writings, whether or not patentable, relating to any art, method, process, machine, manufacture, design or composition of matter, device, system, computer program, or commercial or business method of any kind, or any improvements thereof which, at any time during the period of my employment by the Corporation, relate in any way to the business of the Corporation, or to the machinery, methods, processes and tools used in such business.

3. "Patents"—The term "Patents" as used herein includes: any patent applications relating to said Inventions that may be filed in the United States or any foreign country; any divisions, continuations, continuations-in-part, or substitute applications thereof; any Letters Patent (utility, design or otherwise) which may issue in the United States or any foreign country from any of said applications; and any reissue or renewal Letters Patent based on any of said Letters Patent.

4. My rights to all Inventions which are conceived, reduced to practice, or made by me, either alone or with others, during my employment by the Corporation and during the six (6) months immediately thereafter, either during or outside of my regular working hours, shall belong to the Corporaiton, whether or not the Corporation files for Patents thereon. I will disclose all Inventions promptly, fully, and in writing, to the officials designated by the Corporation, and I agree to assign and do hereby assign all my right, title and interest in and to the Inventions and Patents to the Corporation.

5. During my employment by the Corporation, and at any time thereafter, I will execute all papers and perform all reasonable acts requested by the Corporation for assignment, transfer of interests, preparation, procurement, prosecution, issuance, maintenance and exploitation of the Inventions and Patents.

6. I will regard and preserve as confidential all information pertaining to the business of the Corporation which is obtained by me as a result of employment, including information originated by me and information from specifications, conversations, reports, drawings, hardware, Inventions, or any other source. Except as authorized in writing by the Corporation, I will not disclose any such information to persons outside the Corporation or remove any such information in physical form from the premises of the Corporation.

7. This Agreement shall be binding upon my heirs, administrators, executors and assigns and inure to the benefit of the Corporation and the successors or assigns of all or any part of its business. If any term or portion of this Agreement is held to be legally inapplicable or unenforceable, the remainder of this Agreement shall remain in full force and effect.

8. I do not and will not assert or claim any rights against the Corporation in any existing improvements, inventions, discoveries or patents other than those listed on the reverse side of this Agreement.

EMPLOYEE (PRINT NAME CLEARLY)

EMPLOYEE SIGNATURE

DATE

California Addendum to Assignment of Inventions Agreement

The obligation regarding assignment of rights to inventions as set forth in the C Company Assignment of Inventions Agreement is subject to California Labor Code, Division 3, Chapter 2, Article 3.5 and the limitations in Section 2870 thereof which presently reads as follows:

"2870. Any provision in an employment agreement which provides that an employee shall assign or offer to assign any of his or her rights in an invention to his or her employer shall not apply to an invention for which no equipment, supplies, facility, or trade secret information of the employer was used and which was developed entirely on the employee's own time, and (a) which does not relate (1) to the business of the employer or (2) to the employer's actual or demonstrably anticipated research or development, or (b) which does not result from any work performed by the employee for the employer. Any provision which purports to apply to such an invention is to that extent against the public policy of this state and is to that extent void and unenforceable."

The above limitations shall not apply to inventions required by contract between C and the United States to be assigned to the United States or any of its agencies.

All inventions, including those qualifying under Section 2870 quoted above, which are made by me solely or jointly with others during my term of employment with C shall be disclosed to C for review to determine such issues as may arise under the California Labor Code and the C Assignment of Inventions Agreement.

_____

EMPLOYEE (PRINT NAME CLEARLY)

_____   _____

          DATE   EMPLOYEE SIGNATURE

Criticisms of the C company agreement center around provisions numbered 2 and 4. These provisions are intended to allow the employer to lay claim to every type of idea or invention which the employee may produce or contribute to either during his or her employment or within a six-month period after termination. Inventions are claimed by the employer so long as they relate in any way to its business or even the tools which it uses. The agreement explicitly states that it applies to inventions which are made outside of regular working hours. By this agreement, C company claims idea products which are well beyond the reasonable scope of its own activities and idea products which are in no way related to the employee's activities. These provisions should be recognized as completely unreasonable in their scope. Furthermore, claim to inventions made during the six-month period after the termination of employment is a definite intrusion on the employee's mobility.

On its face, C company agreement would appear to violate the California invention statute. In an effort to address this, C company has provided a "California Addendum." This addendum, however, merely recites the California statute. C company would undoubtedly argue that this recitation meets any objections to the contract based on the California statute, on the basis that these restrictions are effectively deleted because they are void and unenforceable. The trouble with this argument is that it makes the agreement itself extremely vague. The employee who signs this agreement, together with the addendum, will have an impossible task of determining which inventions are his and which are not. Even with the help of a lawyer, the employee will probably remain in the dark.

Because the C company agreement has such broad sweep and contains no provision which attempts to recognize employee rights, I find that it is completely unacceptable. Certainly C company's lawyers will argue to the contrary. However, if it is ever to be enforced, this agreement may have to make it past each and every objection which the employee might make based on chapter 3.

General comments

The foregoing comments have been directed to the contract provisions standing alone. It must be remembered that the interpretation of a contract will ultimately take into account many other factors. The bargaining position of the parties at the time that the contract is signed may show that the agreement was unconscionable.[7] Another possibility is that an employee who is governed by one of these agreements may work in a field where a

---

7. *See* pages 38–42.

great deal of employee mobility is expected. If this is the case, there may be a very strong argument that the particular agreement under those circumstances intrudes too heavily on his or her mobility.[8] The employee might also have an effective argument that the employer gave grossly inadequate compensation under the circumstances.[9]

Finally, the employer should be aware that its true interest lies in encouraging its employees and in generating their enthusiasm. Perhaps the employer will be able to make a respectable legal argument that its agreement can withstand the various objections which are made to it. Even if this were to be the case, the employment contract may be too heavyhanded. If the employment contract is felt to be too heavyhanded, it is very likely that the potential advantages which it may offer in a court of law will be far offset by the costs and disadvantages which it engenders in terms of employee disaffection.

Conclusion

Those who participate in work which produces idea products need to have a basic understanding of the law which governs intellectual property rights and the law which governs the creation of idea products within the employment environment. Generally it is sufficient if both the employer and the employee understand what patents, copyrights, and trade secrets are; and understand the five guidelines of chapter 3. These guidelines are: the importance of the employment contract, the role of good faith in employment relations, the necessity of respecting the essential interests of each party to the employment contract, the impact of job assignments on intellectual property claims, and respect for employer property. One of the roles of an attorney who advises people who work in the idea fields is to coach the client the basic awareness of these necessary items.

In addition, it is important to make realistic plans concerning potential legal conflicts over the ownership of ideas. This planning includes obtaining timely advice and guidance from an attorney. It also includes establishing certain review mechanisms so that legal pitfalls can be avoided.

Adequate planning, together with the continuous efforts of each party to treat the other fairly, will go a long way toward minimizing conflicts over idea products. When conflicts do arise, an early review of the essential interests of the employer and the employee may help to create a reasonable basis for resolution of the dispute. An important overall goal is to create and preserve a productive working environment.[10]

---

8. *See* pages 42–43.
9. *See* page 43.
10. *See* page 43.

Appendix

This appendix is a compilation of the United States statutes, state statutes, and certain other references related to the ownership of idea work. The materials included here are as follows:

1. Selected extracts from the patent statutes of the United States (United States Code, Title 35—Patents). Reprinted with permission from Lawyers Co-operative Publishing Co., Rochester, New York, and Bancroft-Whitney Co., San Francisco, California.
2. Selected extracts from the Copyright Act of the United States (United States Code, Title 17—Copyrights). Reprinted with permission from Lawyers Co-operative Publishing Co., Rochester, New York and Bancroft-Whitney Co., San Francisco, California.
3. Selected extracts from the crime statutes of the United States (United States Code, Title 18—Crimes). Reprinted with permission from Lawyers Co-operative Publishing Co., Rochester, New York and Bancroft-Whitney Co., San Francisco, California.
4. Uniform Trade Secrets Act (adopted by the Commissioners on Uniform State Laws at their 1979 annual conference; adopted in various forms in fifteen states). Reprinted with permission from Uniform Laws Annotated, Copyright 1980 by West Publishing Co.
5. Minnesota Uniform Trade Secrets Act (Minnesota Statutes Annotated Sections 325C.01 to 325C.08). Reprinted with permission from Minnesota Statutes Annotated, Copyright 1981 and 1987 by West Publishing Co.
6. Restatement (First) of Torts, Section 757. Copyright 1945 by the American Law Institute. Reprinted with permission of the American Law Institute.
7. Uniform Commercial Code, Section 2-103. Reprinted with permission from Lawyers Co-operative Publishing Co., Rochester, New York and Bancroft-Whitney Co., San Francisco, California.
8. Uniform Commercial Code, Section 2-302. Reprinted with permission from Lawyers Co-operative Publishing Co., Rochester, New York and Bancroft-Whitney Co., San Francisco, California.
9. Restatement (Second) of Contracts, Section 208. Copyright 1981 by the American Law Institute. Reprinted with permission of the American Law Institute.

10. California Civil Code Section 1670.5. Reprinted with permission from West's Annotated California Codes, Copyright 1973, by West Publishing Co.

11. California Business and Professions Code, Section 16600. Reprinted with permission from West's Annotated California Codes, Copyright 1964, by West Publishing Co.

12. California Labor Code Section 2860. Reprinted with permission from West's Annotated California Codes, Copyright 1971 and 1987 by West Publishing Co.

13. California Labor Code Sections 2870 through 2872. Reprinted with permission from West's Annotated California Codes, Copyright 1971 and 1987 by West Publishing Co.

14. Minnesota Statutes Annotated Section 181.78. Reprinted with permission from Minnesota Statutes Annotated, Copyright 1966 and 1987 by West Publishing Co.

15. Washington Revised Code Sections 49.44.140 through 49.44.150. Reprinted with permission from West's Washington Revised Code Annotated, Copyright 1987, by West Publishing Co.

Selected extracts from the Patent Statutes of the United States

(United States Code, Title 35—Patents)

§ 101. Inventions patentable

Whoever invents or discovers any new and useful process, machine, manufacture, or composition of matter, or any new and useful improvement thereof, may obtain a patent therefor, subject to the conditions and requirements of this title [35 USCS §§ 1 et seq.].
(July 19, 1952, ch 950, § 1, 66 Stat. 797.)

§102. Conditions for patentability; novelty and loss of right to patent

A person shall be entitled to a patent unless—

(a) the invention was known or used by others in this country, or patented or described in a printed publication in this or a foreign country, before the invention thereof by the applicant for patent, or

(b) the invention was patented or described in a printed publication in this or a foreign country or in public use or on sale in this country, more than one year prior to the date of the application for patent in the United States, or

(c) he has abandoned the invention, or

(d) the invention was first patented or caused to be patented, or was the subject of an inventor's certificate, by the applicant or his legal representatives or assigns in a foreign country prior to the date of the application for patent in this country on an application for patent or inventor's certificate filed more than twelve months before the filing of the application in the United States, or

(e) the invention was described in a patent granted on an application for patent by another filed in the United States before the invention thereof by the applicant for patent, or on an international application by another who has fulfilled the requirements of paragraphs (1), (2), and (4) of section 371 (c) of this title [35 USCS § 371(c)(1), (2), (4)] before the invention thereof by the applicant for patent, or

(f) he did not himself invent the subject matter sought to be patented, or

(g) before the applicant's invention thereof the invention was made in this country by another who had not abandoned, suppressed, or concealed it. In determining priority of invention there shall be considered not only the respective dates of conception and reduction to practice of the invention,

but also the reasonable diligence of one who was first to conceive and last to reduce to practice, from a time prior to conception by the other.
(July 19, 1952, ch 950, § 1, 66 Stat. 797; July 28, 1972, P. L. 92-358, § 2, 86 Stat. 502; Nov. 14, 1975, P. L. 94-131, § 5, 89 Stat. 691.)

§ 103.   Conditions for patentability; non-obvious subject matter

A patent may not be obtained though the invention is not identically disclosed or described as set forth in section 102 of this title, if the differences between the subject matter sought to be patented and the prior art are such that the subject matter as a whole would have been obvious at the time the invention was made to a person having ordinary skill in the art to which said subject matter pertains. Patentability shall not be negatived by the manner in which the invention was made.

Subject matter developed by another person, which qualifies as prior art only under subsection (f) or (g) of section 102 of this title [35 USCS § 102(f), (g)], shall not preclude patentability under this section where the subject matter and the claimed invention were, at the time the invention was made, owned by the same person or subject to an obligation of assignment to the same person.
(As amended Nov. 8, 1984, Pub.L. 98-622, Title I, § 103, 98 Stat. 3384.)

§ 111.   Application for patent

Application for patent shall be made, or authorized to be made, by the inventor, except as otherwise provided in this title [35 USCS §§ 1 et seq.], in writing to the Commissioner. Such application shall include (1) a specification as prescribed by section 112 of this title [35 USCS § 112]; (2) a drawing as prescribed by section 113 of this title [35 USCS § 113]; and (3) an oath by the applicant as prescribed by section 115 of this title [35 USCS § 115]. The application must be accompanied by the fee required by law. The fee and oath may be submitted after the specification and any required drawing are submitted, within such period and under such conditions, including the payment of a surcharge, as may be prescribed by the Commissioner. Upon failure to submit the fee and oath within such prescribed period, the application shall be regarded as abandoned, unless it is shown to the satisfaction of the Commissioner that the delay in submitting the fee and oath was unavoidable. The filing date of an application shall be the date on which the specification and any required drawing are received in the Patent and Trademark Office.
(As amended Aug. 27, 1982, P. L. 97-247, § 5, 96 Stat. 319.)

§ 112.   Specification

The specification shall contain a written description of the invention, and of the manner and process of making and using it, in such full, clear, concise, and exact terms as to enable any person skilled in the art to which it pertains, or with which it is most nearly connected, to make and use the same, and shall set forth the best mode contemplated by the inventor of carrying out his invention.

The specification shall conclude with one or more claims particularly pointing out and distinctly claiming the subject matter which the applicant regards as his invention.

A claim may be written in independent or, if the nature of the case admits, in dependent or multiple dependent form.

Subject to the following paragraph, a claim in dependent form shall contain a reference to a claim previously set forth and then specify a further limitation of the subject matter claimed. A claim in dependent form shall be construed to incorporate by reference all the limitations of the claim to which it refers.

A claim in multiple dependent form shall contain a reference, in the alternative only, to more than one claim previously set forth and then specify a further limitation of the subject matter claimed. A multiple dependent claim shall not serve as a basis for any other multiple dependent claim. A multiple claim shall be construed to incorporate by reference all the limitations of the particular claim in relation to which it is being considered.

An element in a claim for a combination may be expressed as a means or step for performing a specified function without the recital of structure, material, or acts in support thereof, and such claim shall be construed to cover the corresponding structure, material, or acts described in the specification and equivalents thereof.
(July 19, 1952, ch 950, § 1, 66 Stat. 798; July 24, 1965, P. L. 89-83, § 9, 79 Stat. 261; Nov. 14, 1975, P. L. 94-131, § 7, 89 Stat. 691.)

§ 118.   Filing by other than inventor

Whenever an inventor refuses to execute an application for patent, or cannot be found or reached after diligent effort, a person to whom the inventor has assigned or agreed in writing to assign the invention or who otherwise shows sufficient proprietary interest in the matter justifying such action, may make application for patent on behalf of and as agent for the inventor on proof of the pertinent facts and a showing that such action is necessary to preserve the rights of the parties or to prevent irreparable damage; and the Commissioner may grant a patent to such inventor upon such notice to him as the Commissioner deems sufficient, and on compliance with such regulations as he prescribes.
(July 19, 1952, ch 950, § 1, 66 Stat. 799.)

§ 151. Issue of patent

If it appears that applicant is entitled to a patent under the law, a written notice of allowance of the application shall be given or mailed to the applicant. The notice shall specify a sum, constituting the issue fee or a portion thereof, which shall be paid within three months thereafter.

Upon payment of this sum the patent shall issue, but if payment is not timely made, the application shall be regarded as abandoned.

Any remaining balance of the issue fee shall be paid within three months from the sending of a notice thereof and, if not paid, the patent shall lapse at the termination of this three-month period. In calculating the amount of a remaining balance, charges for a page or less may be disregarded.

If any payment required by this section is not timely made, but is submitted with the fee for delayed payment and the delay in payment is shown to have been unavoidable, it may be accepted by the Commissioner as though no abandonment or lapse had ever occurred.
(July 19, 1952, ch 950, § 1, 66 Stat. 803; July 24, 1965, P. L. 89-83, § 4, 79 Stat. 260; Jan. 2, 1975, P. L. 93-601, § 3, 88 Stat. 1956.)

§ 154. Contents and term of patent

Every patent shall contain a short title of the invention and a grant to the patentee, his heirs or assigns, for the term of seventeen years, subject to the payment of fees as provided for in this title [35 USCS §§ 1 et seq.], of the right to exclude others from making, using, or selling the invention throughout the United States, referring to the specification for the particulars thereof. A copy of the specification and drawings shall be annexed to the patent and be a part thereof.
(July 19, 1952, ch 950, § 1, 66 Stat. 804; July 24, 1965, P.L. 89-83, § 5, 79 Stat. 261; Dec. 12, 1980, P. L. 96-517, § 4, 94 Stat. 3018.)

§ 173. Term of design patent

Patents for designs shall be granted for the term of fourteen years.
(As amended Aug. 27, 1982, P. L. 97-247, § 16, 96 Stat. 321.)

§ 182. Abandonment of invention for unauthorized disclosure

The invention disclosed in an application for patent subject to an order made pursuant to section 181 of this title [35 USCS § 181] may be held abandoned upon its being established by the Commissioner that in violation of said order the invention has been published or disclosed or that an application for a patent therefor has been filed in a foreign country by the inventor, his successors, assigns, or legal representatives, or anyone in

privity with him or them, without the consent of the Commissioner. The abandonment shall be held to have occurred as of the time of violation. The consent of the Commissioner shall not be given without the concurrence of the heads of the departments and the chief officers of the agencies who caused the order to be issued. A holding of abandonment shall constitute forfeiture by the applicant, his successors, assigns, or legal representatives, or anyone in privity with him or them, of all claims against the United States based upon such invention.
(July 19, 1952, ch 950, § 1, 66 Stat. 806.)

§ 186. Penalty

Whoever, during the period or periods of time an invention has been ordered to be kept secret and the grant of a patent thereon withheld pursuant to section 181 of this title [35 USCS § 181], shall, with knowledge of such order and without due authorization, willfully publish or disclose or authorize or cause to be published or disclosed the invention, or material information with respect thereto, or whoever, in violation of the provisions of section 184 of this title [35 USCS § 184], shall file or cause or authorize to be filed in any foreign country an application for patent or for the registration of a utility model, industrial design, or model in respect of any invention made in the United States, shall, upon conviction, be fined not more than $10,000 or imprisoned for not more than two years, or both.
(July 19, 1952, ch 950, § 1, 66 Stat. 807.)

§ 261. Ownership; assignment

Subject to the provisions of this title [35 USCS §§ 1 et seq.], patents shall have the attributes of personal property.

Applications for patent, patents, or any interest therein, shall be assignable in law by an instrument in writing. The applicant, patentee, or his assigns or legal representatives may in like manner grant and convey an exclusive right under his application for patent, or patents, to the whole or any specified part of the United States.

A certificate of acknowledgment under the hand and official seal of a person authorized to administer oaths within the United States, or, in a foreign country, of a diplomatic or consular officer of the United States or an officer authorized to administer oaths whose authority is proved by a certificate of a diplomatic or consular officer of the United States, or apostille of an official designated by a foreign country which, by treaty or convention, accords like effect to apostilles of designated officials in the United States, shall be prima facie evidence of the execution of an assignment, grant or conveyance of a patent or application for patent.

An assignment, grant or conveyance shall be void as against any subsequent purchaser or mortgagee for a valuable consideration, without notice, unless it is recorded in the Patent and Trademark Office within three months from its date or prior to the date of such subsequent purchase or mortgage. (As amended Aug. 27, 1982, P.L. 97-247, § 14(b), 96 Stat. 321.)

§ 271. Infringement of patent

(a) Except as otherwise provided in this title [35 USCS § 1 et seq.], whoever without authority makes, uses or sells any patented invention, within the United States during the term of the patent therefor, infringes the patent.

(b) Whoever actively induces infringement of a patent shall be liable as an infringer.

(c) Whoever sells a component of a patented machine, manufacture, combination or composition, or a material or apparatus for use in practicing a patented process, constituting a material part of the invention, knowing the same to be especially made or especially adapted for use in an infringement of such patent, and not a staple article or commodity of commerce suitable for substantial noninfringing use, shall be liable as a contributory infringer.

(d) No patent owner otherwise entitled to relief for infringement or contributory infringement of a patent shall be denied relief or deemed guilty of misuse or illegal extension of the patent right by reason of his having done one or more of the following: (1) derived revenue from acts which if performed by another without his consent would constitute contributory infringement of the patent; (2) licensed or authorized another to perform acts which if performed without his consent would constitute contributory infringement of the patent; (3) sought to enforce his patent rights against infringement or contributory infringement.
(July 19, 1952, ch 950, § 1, 66 Stat. 811.)

(e) (1) It shall not be an act of infringement to make, use, or sell a patented invention (other than a new animal drug or veterinary biological product (as those terms are used in the Federal Food, Drug, and Cosmetic Act and the Act of March 4, 1913)) solely for uses reasonably related to the development and submission of information under a Federal law which regulates the manufacture, use, or sale of drugs.

(2) It shall be an act of infringement to submit an application under section 505(j) of the Federal Food, Drug, and Cosmetic Act [21 USCS § 355(j)] or described in section 505(b)(2) of such Act [21 USCS § 355(b)(2)] for a drug claimed in a patent or the use of which is claimed in a patent, if the purpose of such submission is to obtain approval

under such Act to engage in the commercial manufacture, use, or sale of a drug claimed in a patent or the use of which is claimed in a patent before the expiration of such patent.

(3) In any action for patent infringement brought under this section, no injunctive or other relief may be granted which would prohibit the making, using, or selling of a patented invention under paragraph (1).

(4) For an act of infringement described in paragraph (2)—

(A) the court shall order the effective date of any approval of the drug involved in the infringement to be a date which is not earlier than the date of the expiration of the patent which has been infringed,

(B) injunctive relief may be granted against an infringer to prevent the commercial manufacture, use, or sale of an approved drug, and

(C) damages or other monetary relief may be awarded against an infringer only if there has been commercial manufacture, use, or sale of an approved drug.

The remedies prescribed by subparagraphs (A), (B), and (C) are the only remedies which may be granted by a court for an act of infringement described in paragraph (2), except that a court may award attorney fees under section 285 [35 USCS § 285].

(f) (1) Whoever without authority supplies or causes to be supplied in or from the United States all or a substantial portion of the components of a patented invention, where such components are uncombined in whole or in part, in such manner as to actively induce the combination of such components outside of the United States in a manner that would infringe the patent if such combination occurred within the United States, shall be liable as an infringer.

(2) Whoever without authority supplies or causes to be supplied in or from the United States any component of a patented invention that is especially made or especially adapted for use in the invention and not a staple article or commodity of commerce suitable for substantial non-infringing use, where such component is uncombined in whole or in part, knowing that such component is so made or adapted and intending that such component will be combined outside of the United States in a manner that would infringe the patent if such combination occurred within the United States, shall be liable as an infringer.
(As amended Sept. 24, 1984, Pub.L. 98-417, Title II, § 202, 98 Stat. 1603; Nov. 8, 1984, Pub.L. 98-622, Title I, § 101, 98 Stat. 3383.)

§ 282. Presumption of validity; defenses

A patent shall be presumed valid. Each claim of a patent (whether in independent or dependent form) shall be presumed valid independently of the validity of other claims; dependent claims shall be presumed valid even though dependent upon an invalid claim. The burden of establishing invalidity of a patent or any claim thereof shall rest on the party asserting it.

The following shall be defenses in any action involving the validity or infringement of a patent and shall be pleaded:

(1) Noninfringement, absence of liability for infringement or unenforceability,

(2) Invalidity of the patent or any claim in suit on any ground specified in part II of this title [35 USCS §§ 100 et seq.] as a condition for patentability,

(3) Invalidity of the patent or any claim in suit for failure to comply with any requirement of sections 112 or 251 of this title [35 USCS § 112 or 251],

(4) Any other fact or act made a defense by this title [35 USCS §§ 1 et seq.].

In actions involving the validity or infringement of a patent the party asserting invalidity or noninfringement shall give notice in the pleadings or otherwise in writing to the adverse party at least thirty days before the trial, of the country, number, date, and name of the patentee of any patent, the title, date, and page numbers of any publication to be relied upon as anticipation of the patent in suit or, except in actions in the United States Claims Court, as showing the state of the art, and the name and address of any person who may be relied upon as the prior inventor or as having prior knowledge of or as having previously used or offered for sale the invention of the patent in suit. In the absence of such notice proof of the said matters may not be made at the trial except on such terms as the court requires. Invalidity of the extension of a patent term or any portion thereof under section 156 of this title [35 USCS § 156] because of the material failure—

(1) by the applicant for the extension, or

(2) by the Commissioner,

to comply with the requirements of such section shall be a defense in any action involving the infringement of a patent during the period of the extension of its term and shall be pleaded. A due diligence determination under section 156(d)(2) [35 USCS § 156] is not subject to review in such an action.
(As amended Apr. 2, 1982, P.L. 97-164, Title I, Part B, § 161 (7), 96 Stat. 49; Sept. 24, 1984, Pub.L. 98-417, Title II, § 203, 98 Stat. 1603.)

§ 292. False marking

(a) Whoever, without the consent of the patentee, marks upon, or affixes to, or uses in advertising in connection with anything made, used, or sold by him, the name or any imitation of the name of the patentee, the patent number, or the words "patent," "patentee," or the like, with the intent of counterfeiting or imitating the mark of the patentee, or of deceiving the public and inducing them to believe that the thing was made or sold by or with the consent of the patentee; or

Whoever marks upon, or affixes to, or uses in advertising in connection with any unpatented article, the word "patent" or any word or number importing that the same is patented, for the purpose of deceiving the public; or

Whoever marks upon, or affixes to, or uses in advertising in connection with any article, the words "patent applied for," "patent pending," or any word importing that an application for patent has been made, when no application for patent has been made, or if made, is not pending, for the purpose of deceiving the public—

Shall be fined not more than $500 for every such offense.

(b) Any person may sue for the penalty, in which event one-half shall go to the person suing and the other to the use of the United States.
(July 19, 1952, ch 950, § 1, 66 Stat. 814.)

Selected Extracts from the Copyright Act of the United States
(United States Code, Title 17—Copyrights)

§ 101. Definitions

As used in this title [17 USCS §§ 101 et seq.], the following terms and their variant forms mean the following:

An "anonymous work" is a work on the copies or phonorecords of which no natural person is identified as author.

"Audiovisual works" are works that consist of a series of related images which are intrinsically intended to be shown by the use of machines or devices such as projectors, viewers, or electronic equipment, together with accompanying sounds, if any, regardless of the nature of the material objects, such as films or tapes, in which the works are embodied.

The "best edition" of a work is the edition, published in the United States at any time before the date of deposit, that the Library of Congress determines to be most suitable for its purposes.

A person's "children" are that person's immediate offspring, whether legitimate or not, and any children legally adopted by that person.

A "collective work" is a work, such as a periodical issue, anthology, or encyclopedia, in which a number of contributions, constituting separate and independent works in themselves, are assembled into a collective whole.

A "compilation" is a work formed by the collection and assembling of preexisting materials or of data that are selected, coordinated, or arranged in such a way that the resulting work as a whole constitutes an original work of authorship. The term "compilation" includes collective works.

A "computer program" is a set of statements or instructions to be used directly or indirectly in a computer in order to bring about a certain result. (As amended Dec. 12, 1980, P. L. 96-517, § 10(a), 94 Stat. 3028.)

"Copies" are material objects, other than phonorecords, in which a work is fixed by any method now known or later developed, and from which the work can be perceived, reproduced, or otherwise communicated, either directly or with the aid of a machine or device. The term "copies" includes the material object, other than a phonorecord, in which the work is first fixed.

"Copyright owner," with respect to any one of the exclusive rights comprised in a copyright, refers to the owner of that particular right.

A work is "created" when it is fixed in a copy or phonorecord for the first time; where a work is prepared over a period of time, the portion of it that has been fixed at any particular time constitutes the work as of that time, and where the work has been prepared in different versions, each version constitutes a separate work.

A "derivative work" is a work based upon one or more preexisting works, such as a translation, musical arrangement, dramatization, fictionalization, motion picture version, sound recording, art reproduction, abridgment, condensation, or any other form in which a work may be recast, transformed, or adapted. A work consisting of editorial revisions, annotations, elaborations, or other modifications which, as a whole, represent an original work of authorship, is a "derivative work."

A "device," "machine," or "process" is one now known or later developed.

To "display" a work means to show a copy of it, either directly or by means of a film, slide, television image, or any other device or process or, in the case of a motion picture or other audiovisual work, to show individual images nonsequentially.

A work is "fixed" in a tangible medium of expression when its embodiment in a copy or phonorecord, by or under the authority of the author, is sufficiently permanent or stable to permit it to be perceived, reproduced, or otherwise communicated for a period of more than transitory duration. A work consisting of sounds, images, or both, that are being transmitted, is "fixed" for purposes of this title [17 USCS §§ 101 et seq.] if a fixation of the work is being made simultaneously with its transmission.

The terms "including" and "such as" are illustrative and not limitative.

A "joint work" is a work prepared by two or more authors with the intention that their contributions be merged into inseparable or interdependent parts of a unitary whole.

"Literary works" are works, other than audiovisual works, expressed in words, numbers, or other verbal or numerical symbols or indicia, regardless of the nature of the material objects, such as books, periodicals, manuscripts, phonorecords, film, tapes, disks, or cards, in which they are embodied.

"Motion pictures" are audiovisual works consisting of a series of related images which, when shown in succession, impart an impression of motion, together with accompanying sounds, if any.

To "perform" a work means to recite, render, play, dance, or act it, either directly or by means of any device or process or, in the case of a motion picture or other audiovisual work, to show its images in any sequence or to make the sounds accompanying it audible.

"Phonorecords" are material objects in which sounds, other than those accompanying a motion picture or other audiovisual work, are fixed by any method now known or later developed, and from which the sounds can be perceived, reproduced, or otherwise communicated, either directly or with the aid of a machine or device. The term "phonorecords" includes the material object in which the sounds are first fixed.

"Pictorial, graphic, and sculptural works" include two-dimensional and three-dimensional works of fine, graphic, and applied art, photographs, prints and art reproductions, maps, globes, charts, technical drawings, diagrams, and models. Such works shall include works of artistic crafts-manship insofar as their form but not their mechanical or utilitarian aspects are concerned; the design of a useful article, as defined in this section, shall be considered a pictorial, graphic, or sculptural work only if, and only to the extent that, such design incorporates pictorial, graphic, or sculptural features that can be identified separately from, and are capable of existing independently of, the utilitarian aspects of the article.

A "pseudonymous work" is a work on the copies or phonorecords of which the author is identified under a fictitious name.

"Publication" is the distribution of copies or phonorecords of a work to the public by sale or other transfer of ownership, or by rental, lease, or lending. The offering to distribute copies or phonorecords to a group of persons for purposes of further distribution, public performance, or public display, constitutes publication. A public performance or display of a work does not of itself constitute publication.

To perform or display a work "publicly" means—

(1) to perform or display it at a place open to the public or at any place where a substantial number of persons outside of a normal circle of a family and its social acquaintances is gathered; or

(2) to transmit or otherwise communicate a performance or display of the work to a place specified by clause (1) or to the public, by means of any device or process, whether the members of the public capable of receiving the performance or display receive it in the same place or in separate places and at the same time or at different times.

"Sound recordings" are works that result from the fixation of a series of musical, spoken, or other sounds, but not including the sounds accompanying a motion picture or other audiovisual work, regardless of the nature of the material objects, such as disks, tapes, or other phonorecords, in which they are embodied.

"State" includes the District of Columbia and the Commonwealth of Puerto Rico, and any territories to which this title [17 USCS §§ 101 et seq.] is made applicable by an Act of Congress.

A "transfer of copyright ownership" is an assignment, mortgage, exclusive license, or any other conveyance, alienation, or hypothecation of a copyright or of any of the exclusive rights comprised in a copyright, whether or not it is limited in time or place of effect, but not including a nonexclusive license.

A "transmission program" is a body of material that, as an aggregate, has been produced for the sole purpose of transmission to the public in sequence and as a unit.

To "transmit" a performance or display is to communicate it by any device or process whereby images or sounds are received beyond the place from which they are sent.

The "United States", when used in a geographical sense, comprises the several States, the District of Columbia and the Commonwealth of Puerto Rico, and the organized territories under the jurisdiction of the United States Government.

A "useful article" is an article having an intrinsic utilitarian function that is not merely to portray the appearance of the article or to convey information. An article that is normally a part of a useful article is considered a "useful article."

The author's "widow" or "widower" is the author's surviving spouse under the law of the author's domicile at the time of his or her death, whether or not the spouse has later remarried.

A "work of the United States Government" is a work prepared by an officer or employee of the United States Government as part of that person's official duties.

A "work made for hire" is—

(1) a work prepared by an employee within the scope of his or her employment; or

(2) a work specially ordered or commissioned for use as a contribution to a collective work, as a part of a motion picture or other audiovisual work, as a translation, as a supplementary work, as a compilation, as an instructional text, as a test, as answer material for a test, or as an atlas, if the parties expressly agree in a written instrument signed by them that the work shall be considered a work made for hire. For the purpose of the foregoing sentence, a "supplementary work" is a work prepared for publication as a secondary adjunct to a work by another author for the purpose of introducing, concluding, illustrating, explaining, revising, commenting upon, or assisting in the use of the other work, such as forewords, afterwords, pictorial illustrations, maps, charts, tables, editorial notes, musical arrangements, answer material for tests, bibliographies, appendixes, and indexes, and an "instructional text" is a literary, pictorial, or graphic work prepared for publication and with the purpose of use in systematic instructional activities.

A "computer program" is a set of statements or instructions to be used directly or indirectly in a computer in order to bring about a certain result. (As amended Dec. 12, 1980, P.L. 96-517, § 10(a), 94 lStat. 3028.)

§ 102.   Subject matter of copyright: In general

(a) Copyright protection subsists, in accordance with this title [17 USCS §§ 101 et seq.], in original works of authorship fixed in any tangible medium of expression, now known or later developed, from which they can be perceived, reproduced, or otherwise communicated, either directly or with the aid of a machine or device. Works of authorship include the following categories:

> (1) literary works;
> (2) musical works, including any accompanying words;
> (3) dramatic works, including any accompanying music;
> (4) pantomimes and choreographic works;
> (5) pictorial, graphic, and sculptural works;
> (6) motion pictures and other audiovisual works; and
> (7) sound recordings.

(b) In no case does copyright protection for an original work of authorship extend to any idea, procedure, process, system, method of operation, concept, principle, or discovery, regardless of the form in which it is described, explained, illustrated, or embodied in such work.
(Added Oct. 19, 1976, P. L. 94-553, Title I, § 101, 90 Stat 2544.)

§ 104.   Subject matter of copyright: National origin

(a) Unpublished works.

The works specified by sections 102 and 103 [17 USCS §§ 102 and 103], while unpublished, are subject to protection under this title [17 USCS §§ 101 et seq.] without regard to the nationality or domicile of the author.

(b) Published works.

The works specified by sections 102 and 103 [17 USCS §§ 102 and 103], when published, are subject to protection under this title [17 USCS §§ 101 et seq.] if—

> (1) on the date of first publication, one or more of the authors is a national or domiciliary of the United States, or is a national, domiciliary, or sovereign authority of a foreign nation that is a party to a copyright treaty to which the United States is also a party, or is a stateless person, wherever that person may be domiciled; or

> (2) the work is first published in the United States or in a foreign nation that, on the date of first publication, is a party to the Universal Copyright Convention; or

(3) the work is first published by the United Nations or any of its specialized agencies, or by the Organization of American States; or

(4) the work comes within the scope of a Presidential proclamation. Whenever the President finds that a particular foreign nation extends, to works by authors who are nationals or domiciliaries of the United States or to works that are first published in the United States, copyright protection on substantially the same basis as that on which the foreign nation extends protection to works of its own nationals and domiciliaries and works first published in that nation, the President may by proclamation extend protection under this title [17 USCS §§ 101 et seq.] to works of which one or more of the authors is, on the date of first publication, a national, domiciliary, or sovereign authority of that nation, or which was first published in that nation. The President may revise, suspend, or revoke any such proclamation or impose any conditions or limitations on protection under a proclamation.

(Added Oct. 19, 1976, P. L. 94-553, Title I, § 101, 90 Stat 2545.)

§ 106. Exclusive rights in copyrighted works

Subject to sections 107 through 118 [17 USCS §§ 107–118], the owner of copyright under this title [17 USCS §§ 101 et seq.] has the exclusive rights to do and to authorize any of the following:

(1) to reproduce the copyrighted work in copies or phonorecords;
(2) to prepare derivative works based upon the copyrighted work;
(3) to distribute copies or phonorecords of the copyrighted work to the public by sale or other transfer of ownership, or by rental, lease or lending;
(4) in the case of literary, musical, dramatic, and choreographic works, pantomimes, and motion pictures and other audiovisual works, to perform the copyrighted work publicly; and
(5) in the case of literary, musical, dramatic, and choreographic works, pantomimes, and pictorial, graphic, or sculptural works, including the individual images of a motion picture or other audiovisual work, to display the copyrighted work publicly.

(Added Oct. 19, 1976, P. L. 94-553, Title I, § 101, 90 Stat 2546.)

§ 107. Limitations on exclusive rights: Fair use

Notwithstanding the provisions of section 106 [17 USCS § 106], the fair use of a copyrighted work, including such use by reproduction in copies or phonorecords or by any other means specified by that section, for purposes such as criticism, comment, news reporting, teaching (including multiple copies for classroom use), scholarship, or research, is not an infringement of copyright. In determining whether the use made of a work in any particular case is a fair use the factors to be considered shall include—

> (1) the purpose and character of the use, including whether such use is of a commercial nature or is for nonprofit educational purposes;
> (2) the nature of the copyrighted work;
> (3) the amount and substantiality of the portion used in relation to the copyrighted work as a whole; and
> (4) the effect of the use upon the potential market for or value of the copyrighted work.

(Added Oct. 19, 1976, P. L. 94-553, Title I, § 101, 90 Stat. 2546.)

§ 117.   Limitations on exclusive rights: Computer programs

Notwithstanding the provisions of section 106 [17 USCS § 106], it is not an infringement for the owner of a copy of a computer program to make or authorize the making of another copy or adaptation of that computer program provided:

> (1) that such a new copy or adaptation is created as an essential step in the utilization of the computer program in conjunction with a machine and that it is used in no other manner, or
> (2) that such new copy or adaptation is for archival purposes only and that all archival copies are destroyed in the event that continued possession of the computer program should cease to be rightful.

> Any exact copies prepared in accordance with the provisions of this section may be leased, sold, or otherwise transferred, along with the copy from which such copies were prepared, only as part of the lease, sale, or other transfer of all rights in the program. Adaptations so prepared may be transferred only with the authorization of the copyright owner.

(As amended Dec. 12, 1980, P. L. 96-517, § 10(b), 94 Stat. 3028.)

§ 201.   Ownership of copyright

(a) **Initial ownership.** Copyright in a work protected under this title [17 USCS §§ 101 et seq.] vests initially in the author or authors of the work. The authors of a joint work are co-owners of copyright in the work.

(b) **Works made for hire.** In the case of a work made for hire, the employer or other person for whom the work was prepared is considered the author for purposes of this title [17 USCS §§ 101 et seq.], and, unless the parties have expressly agreed otherwise in a written instrument signed by them, owns all of the rights comprised in the copyright.

(c) Contributions to collective works. Copyright in each separate contribution to a collective work is distinct from copyright in the collective work as a whole, and vests initially in the author of the contribution. In the absence of an express transfer of the copyright or of any rights under it, the owner of copyright in the collective work is presumed to have acquired only the privilege of reproducing and distributing the contribution as part of that particular collective work, any revision of that collective work, and any later collective work in the same series.

(d) Transfer of ownership. (1) The ownership of a copyright may be transferred in whole or in part by any means of conveyance or by operation of law, and may be bequeathed by will or pass as personal property by the applicable laws of intestate succession.

(2) Any of the exclusive rights comprised in a copyright, including any subdivision of any of the rights specified by section 106 [17 USCS § 106], may be transferred as provided by clause (1) and owned separately. The owner of any particular exclusive right is entitled, to the extent of that right, to all of the protection and remedies accorded to the copyright owner by this title [17 USCS §§ 101 et seq.].

(e) Involuntary transfer. When an individual author's ownership of a copyright, or of any of the exclusive rights under a copyright, has not previously been transferred voluntarily by that individual author, no action by any governmental body or other official or organization purporting to seize, expropriate, transfer, or exercise rights of ownership with respect to the copyright, or any of the exclusive rights under a copyright, shall be given effect under this title [17 USCS §§ 101 et seq.], except as provided under title 11 [11 USCS §§ 1 et seq.].

(As amended Nov. 6, 1978, P. L. 95-598, Title III, § 313, 92 Stat. 2676.)

§ 202. Ownership of copyright as distinct from ownership of material object

Ownership of a copyright, or of any of the exclusive rights under a copyright, is distinct from ownership of any material object in which the work is embodied. Transfer of ownership of any material object, including the copy or phonorecord in which the work is first fixed, does not of itself convey any rights in the copyrighted work embodied in the object; nor, in the absence of an agreement, does transfer of ownership of a copyright or of any exclusive rights under a copyright convey property rights in any material object.

(Added Oct. 19, 1976, P. L. 94-553, Title I, § 101, 90 Stat. 2568.)

§ 204. Execution of transfers of copyright ownership

(a) A transfer of copyright ownership, other than by operation of law, is not valid unless an instrument of conveyance, or a note or memorandum of the transfer, is in writing and signed by the owner of the rights conveyed or such owner's duly authorized agent.

(b) A certificate of acknowledgement is not required for the validity of a transfer, but is prima facie evidence of the execution of the transfer if—

> (1) in the case of a transfer executed in the United States, the certificate is issued by a person authorized to administer oaths within the United States; or
> (2) in the case of a transfer executed in a foreign country, the certificate is issued by a diplomatic or consular officer of the United States, or by a person authorized to administer oaths whose authority is proved by a certificate of such an officer.

(Added Oct. 19, 1976, P. L. 94-553, Title I, § 101, 90 Stat. 2570.)

§ 301. Preemption with respect to other laws

(a) On and after January 1, 1978, all legal or equitable rights that are equivalent to any of the exclusive rights within the general scope of copyright as specified by section 106 [17 USCS § 106] in works of authorship that are fixed in a tangible medium of expression and come within the subject matter of copyright as specified by sections 102 and 103 [17 USCS §§ 102 and 103], whether created before or after that date and whether published or unpublished, are governed exclusively by this title [17 USCS §§ 101 et seq.]. Thereafter, no person is entitled to any such right or equivalent right in any such work under the common law or statutes of any State.

(b) Nothing in this title [17 USCS §§ 101 et seq.] annuls or limits any rights or remedies under the common law or statutes of any State with respect to—

> (1) subject matter that does not come within the subject matter of copyright as specified by sections 102 and 103 [17 USCS §§ 102 and 103], including works of authorship not fixed in any tangible medium of expression; or
> (2) any cause of action arising from undertakings commenced before January 1, 1978; or
> (3) activities violating legal or equitable rights that are not equivalent to any of the exclusive rights within the general scope of copyright as specified by section 106 [17 USCS § 106].

(c) With respect to sound recordings fixed before February 15, 1972, any rights or remedies under the common law or statutes of any State shall not be annulled or limited by this title [17 USCS §§ 101 et seq.] until February 15, 2047. The preemptive provisions of subsection (a) shall apply to any such rights and remedies pertaining to any cause of action arising from undertakings commenced on and after February 15, 2047. Notwithstanding the provisions of section 303 [17 USCS § 303], no sound recording fixed before February 15, 1972, shall be subject to copyright under this title [17 USCS §§ 101 et seq.] before, on, or after February 15, 2047.

(d) Nothing in this title [17 USCS §§ 101 et seq.] annuls or limits any rights or remedies under any other Federal statute.
(Added Oct. 19, 1976, P. L. 94-553, Title I, § 101, 90 Stat. 2572.)

§ 302. Duration of copyright: Works created on or after January 1, 1978

(a) In general. Copyright in a work created on or after January 1, 1978, subsists from its creation and, except as provided by the following subsections, endures for a term consisting of the life of the author and fifty years after the author's death.

(b) Joint works. In the case of a joint work prepared by two or more authors who did not work for hire, the copyright endures for a term consisting of the life of the last surviving author and fifty years after such last surviving author's death.

(c) Anonymous works, pseudonymous works, and works made for hire. In the case of an anonymous work, a pseudonymous work, or a work made for hire, the copyright endures for a term of seventy-five years from the year of its first publication, or a term of one hundred years from the year of its creation, whichever expires first. If, before the end of such term, the identity of one or more of the authors of an anonymous or pseudonymous work is revealed in the records of a registration made for that work under subsections (a) or (d) of section 408 [17 USCS § 408], or in the records provided by this subsection, the copyright in the work endures for the term specified by subsection (a) or (b), based on the life of the author or authors whose identity has been revealed. Any person having an interest in the copyright in an anonymous or pseudonymous work may at any time record, in records to be maintained by the Copyright Office for that purpose, a statement identifying one or more authors of the work; the statement shall also identify the person filing it, the nature of that person's interest, the source of the information recorded, and the particular work affected, and shall comply in form and content with requirements that the Register of Copyrights shall prescribe by regulation.

(d) Records relating to death of authors. Any person having an interest in a copyright may at any time record in the Copyright Office a statement of the date of death of the author of the copyrighted work, or a statement that the author is still living on a particular date. The statement shall identify the person filing it, the nature of that person's interest, and the source of the information recorded, and shall comply in form and content with requirements that the Register of Copyrights shall prescribe by regulation. The Register shall maintain current records of information relating to the death of authors of copyrighted works, based on such recorded statements and, to the extent the Register considers practicable, on data contained in any of the records of the Copyright Office or in other reference sources.

(e) Presumption as to author's death. After a period of seventy-five years from the year of first publication of a work, or a period of one hundred years from the year of its creation, whichever expires first, any person who obtains from the Copyright Office a certified report that the records provided by subsection (d) disclose nothing to indicate that the author of the work is living, or died less than fifty years before, is entitled to the benefit of a presumption that the author has been dead for at least fifty years. Reliance in good faith upon this presumption shall be a complete defense to any action for infringement under this title [17 USCS §§ 101 et seq.].
(Added Oct. 19, 1976, P. L. 94-553, Title I, § 101, 90 Stat. 2572.)

§ 401. Notice of copyright: Visually perceptible copies

(a) General requirement. Whenever a work protected under this title [17 USCS §§ 101 et seq.] is published in the United States or elsewhere by authority of the copyright owner, a notice of copyright as provided by this section shall be placed on all publicly distributed copies from which the work can be visually perceived, either directly or with the aid of a machine or device.

(b) Form of notice. The notice appearing on the copies shall consist of the following three elements:

(1) the symbol © (the letter C in a circle), or the word "Copyright", or the abbreviation "Copr."; and

(2) the year of first publication of the work; in the case of compilations or derivative works incorporating previously published material, the year date of first publication of the compilation or derivative work is sufficient. The year date may be omitted where a pictorial, graphic, or sculptural work, with accompanying text matter, if any, is reproduced in or on greeting cards, postcards, stationery, jewelry, dolls, toys, or any useful articles; and

(3) the name of the owner of copyright in the work, or an abbreviation by which the name can be recognized, or a generally known alternative designation of the owner.

(c) Position of notice. The notice shall be affixed to the copies in such manner and location as to give reasonable notice of the claim of copyright.

The Register of Copyrights shall prescribe by regulation, as examples, specific methods of affixation and positions of the notice on various types of works that will satisfy this requirement, but these specifications shall not be considered exhaustive.
(Added Oct. 19, 1976, P. L. 94-553, Title I, § 101, 90 Stat. 2576.)

§ 408. Copyright registration in general

(a) Registration permissive. At any time during the subsistence of copyright in any published or unpublished work, the owner of copyright or of any exclusive right in the work may obtain registration of the copyright claim by delivering to the Copyright Office the deposit specified by this section, together with the application and fee specified by sections 409 and 708 [17 USCS §§ 409 and 708]. Subject to the provisions of section 405(a) [17 USCS § 405(a)], such registration is not a condition of copyright protection.

(b) Deposit for copyright registration. Except as provided by subsection (c), the material deposited for registration shall include—

(1) in the case of an unpublished work, one complete copy or phonorecord;
(2) in the case of a published work, two complete copies or phonorecords of the best edition;
(3) in the case of a work first published outside the United States, one complete copy or phonorecord as so published;
(4) in the case of a contribution to a collective work, one complete copy or phonorecord of the best edition of the collective work.

Copies or phonorecords deposited for the Library of Congress under section 407 [17 USCS § 407] may be used to satisfy the deposit provisions of this section, if they are accompanied by the prescribed application and fee, and by any additional identifying material that the Register may, by regulation, require. The Register shall also prescribe regulations establishing requirements under which copies or phonorecords acquired for the Library of Congress under subsection (e) of section 407 [17 USCS § 407(e)], otherwise than by deposit, may be used to satisfy the deposit provisions of this section.

(c) Administrative classification and optional deposit.

(1) The Register of Copyrights is authorized to specify by regulation the administrative classes into which works are to be placed for purposes of deposit and registration, and the nature of the copies or phonorecords to be deposited in the various classes specified.

The regulations may require or permit, for particular classes, the deposit of identifying material instead of copies or phonorecords, the deposit of only one copy or phonorecord where two would normally be required, or a single registration for a group of related works. This administrative classification of works has no significance with respect to the subject matter of copyright or the exclusive rights provided by this title [17 USCS § 408].

(2) Without prejudice to the general authority provided under clause (1), the Register of Copyrights shall establish regulations specifically permitting a single registration for a group of works by the same individual author, all first published as contributions to periodicals, including newspapers, within a twelve-month period, on the basis of a single deposit, application, and registration fee, under all of the following conditions—

(A) if each of the works as first published bore a separate copyright notice, and the name of the owner of copyright in the work, or an abbreviation by which the name can be recognized, or a generally known alternative designation of the owner was the same in each notice; and

(B) if the deposit consists of one copy of the entire issue of the periodical, or of the entire section in the case of a newspaper, in which each contribution was first published; and

(C) if the application identifies each work separately, including the periodical containing it and its date of first publication.

(3) As an alternative to separate renewal registrations under subsection (a) of section 304 [17 USCS § 304(a)], a single renewal registration may be made for a group of works by the same individual author, all first published as contributions to periodicals, including newspapers, upon the filing of a single application and fee, under all of the following conditions:

(A) the renewal claimant or claimants, and the basis of claim or claims under section 304(a) [17 USCS § 034(a)], is the same for each of the works; and

(B) the works were all copyrighted upon their first publication, either through separate copyright notice and registration or by virtue of a general copyright notice in the periodical issue as a whole; and

(C) the renewal application and fee are received not more than twenty-eight or less than twenty-seven years after the thirty-first day of December of the calendar year in which all of the works were first published; and

(D) the renewal application identifies each work separately, including the periodical containing it and its date of first publication.

(d) Corrections and amplifications. The Register may also establish, by regulation, formal procedures for the filing of an application for supplementary registration, to correct an error in a copyright registration or to amplify the information given in a registration. Such application shall be accompanied by the fee provided by section 708 [17 USCS § 708], and shall clearly identify the registration to be corrected or amplified. The information contained in a supplementary registration augments but does not supersede that contained in the earlier registration.

(e) Published edition of previously registered work. Registration for the first published edition of a work previously registered in unpublished form may be made even though the work as published is substantially the same as the unpublished version.
(Added Oct. 19, 1976, P. L. 94-553, Title I, § 101, 90 Stat. 2580.)

§ 410. Registration of claim and issuance of certificate

(a) When, after examination, the Register of Copyrights determines that, in accordance with the provisions of this title [17 USCS §§ 101 et seq.], the material deposited constitutes copyrightable subject matter and that the other legal and formal requirements of this title [17 USCS §§ 101 et seq.] have been met, the Register shall register the claim and issue to the applicant a certificate of registration under the seal of the Copyright Office. The certificate shall contain the information given in the application, together with the number and effective date of the registration.

(b) In any case in which the Register of Copyrights determines that, in accordance with the provisions of this title [17 USCS §§ 101 et seq.], the material deposited does not constitute copyrightable subject matter or that the claim is invalid for any other reason, the Register shall refuse registration and shall notify the applicant in writing of the reasons for such refusal.

(c) In any judicial proceedings the certificate of a registration made before or within five years after first publication of the work shall constitute prima facie evidence of the validity of the copyright and of the facts stated in the certificate. The evidentiary weight to be accorded the certificate of a registration made thereafter shall be within the discretion of the court.

(d) The effective date of a copyright registration is the day on which an application, deposit, and fee, which are later determined by the Register of Copyrights or by a court of competent jurisdiction to be acceptable for registration, have all been received in the Copyright Office.
(Added Oct. 19, 1976, P. L. 94-553, Title I, § 101, 90 Stat. 2582.)

§ 411.   Registration as prerequisite to infringement suit

(a) Subject to the provisions of subsection (b), no action for infringement of the copyright in any work shall be instituted until registration of the copyright claim has been made in accordance with this title [17 USCS §§ 101 et seq.]. In any case, however, where the deposit, application, and fee required for registration have been delivered to the Copyright Office in proper form and registration has been refused, the applicant is entitled to institute an action for infringement if notice thereof, with a copy of the complaint, is served on the Register of Copyrights. The Register may, at his or her option, become a party to the action with respect to the issue of registrability of the copyright claim by entering an appearance within sixty days after such service, but the Register's failure to become a party shall not deprive the court of jurisdiction to determine that issue.

(b) In the case of a work consisting of sounds, images, or both, the first fixation of which is made simultaneously with its transmission, the copyright owner may, either before or after such fixation takes place, institute an action for infringement under section 501 [17 USCS § 501], fully subject to the remedies provided by sections 502 through 506 and sections 509 and 510 [17 USCS §§ 502–506, 509, 510], if, in accordance with requirements that the Register of Copyrights shall prescribe by regulation, the copyright owner—

(1) serves notice upon the infringer, not less than ten or more than thirty days before such fixation, identifying the work and the specific time and source of its first transmission, and declaring an intention to secure copyright in the work; and
(2) makes registration for the work within three months after its first transmission.

(Added Oct. 19, 1976, P. L. 94-553, Title I, § 101, 90 Stat. 2583.)

§ 501.   Infringement of copyright

(a) Anyone who violates any of the exclusive rights of the copyright owner as provided by sections 106 through 118 [17 USCS §§ 106–118], or who imports copies or phonorecords into the United States in violation of section 602 [17 USCS § 602], is an infringer of the copyright.

(b) The legal or beneficial owner of an exclusive right under a copyright is entitled, subject to the requirements of sections 205(d) and 411 [17 USCS §§ 205(d) and 411], to institute an action for any infringement of that particular right committed while he or she is the owner of it. The court may require such owner to serve written notice of the action with a copy of the complaint upon any person shown, by the records of the Copyright Office or otherwise, to have or claim an interest in the copyright, and shall require that such notice be served upon any person whose interest is likely to be affected by a decision in the case. The court may require the joinder, and shall permit the intervention, of any person having or claiming an interest in the copyright.

(c) For any secondary transmission by a cable system that embodies a performance or a display of a work which is actionable as an act of infringement under subsection (c) of section 111 [17 USCS § 111(c)], a television broadcast station holding a copyright or other license to transmit or perform the same version of that work shall, for purposes of subsection (b) of this section, be treated as a legal or beneficial owner if such secondary transmission occurs within the local service area of that television station.

(d) For any secondary transmission by a cable system that is actionable as an act of infringement pursuant to section 111(c)(3) [17 USCS § 111(c)(3)], the following shall also have standing to sue: (i) the primary transmitter, whose transmission has been altered by the cable system; and (ii) any broadcast station within whose local service area the secondary transmission occurs.
(Added Oct. 19, 1976, P. L. 94-553, Title I, § 101, 90 Stat. 2584.)

§ 506. Criminal offenses

(a) Criminal infringement. Any person who infringes a copyright willfully and for purposes of commercial advantage or private financial gain shall be punished as provided in section 2319 of title 18 [18 USCS § 2319].

(b) Forfeiture and destruction. When any person is convicted of any violation of subsection (a), the court in its judgment of conviction shall, in addition to the penalty therein prescribed, order the forfeiture and destruction or other disposition of all infringing copies or phonorecords and all implements, devices, or equipment used in the manufacture of such infringing copies or phonorecords.

(c) Fraudulent copyright notice. Any person who, with fraudulent intent, places on any article a notice of copyright or words of the same purport that such person knows to be false, or who, with fraudulent intent, publicly distributes or imports for public distribution any article bearing such notice or words that such person knows to be false, shall be fined not more than $2,500.

(d) Fraudulent removal of copyright notice. Any person who, with fraudulent intent, removes or alters any notice of copyright appearing on a copy of a copyrighted work shall be fined not more than $2,500.

(e) False representation. Any person who knowingly makes a false representation of a material fact in the application for copyright registration provided for by section 409 [17 USCS § 409], or in any written statement filed in connection with the application, shall be fined not more than $2,500. (As amended May 24, 1982, P.L. 97-180, § 5, 96 Stat. 93.)

Selected extracts from the Crimes Statutes of the United States

(United States Code, Title 18—Crimes)

§ 2319. Criminal infringement of a copyright

(a) Whoever violates section 506(a) (relating to criminal offenses) of title 17 [17 USCS § 506(a)], shall be punished as provided in subsection (b) of this section and such penalties shall be in addition to any other provisions of title 17 [17 USCS §§ 101 et seq.] or any other law.

(b) Any person who commits an offense under subsection (a) of this section—

(1) shall be fined not more than $250,000 or imprisoned for not more than five years, or both, if the offense—

(A) involves the reproduction or distribution, during any one-hundred-and-eighty-day period, of at least one thousand phono-records or copies infringing the copyright in one or more sound recordings;

(B) involves the reproduction or distribution, during any one-hundred-and-eighty-day period, of at least sixty-five copies infringing the copyright in one or more motion pictures or other audiovisual works; or

(C) is a second or subsequent offense under either of subsection (b)(1) or (b)(2) of this section, where a prior offense involved a sound recording, or a motion picture or other audiovisual work;

(2) shall be fined not more than $250,000 or imprisoned for not more than two years, or both, if the offense—

(A) involves the reproduction or distribution, during any one-hundred-and-eighty-day period, of more than one hundred but less than one thousand phonorecords or copies infringing the copyright in one or more sound recordings; or

(B) involves the reproduction or distribution, during any one-hundred-and-eighty-day period, of more than seven but less than sixty-five copies infringing the copyright in one or more motion pictures or other audiovisual works; and

(3) shall be fined not more than $25,000 or imprisoned for not more than one year, or both in any other case.

(c) As used in this section—

(1) the terms "sound recording," "motion picture," "audiovisual work," "phonorecord," and "copies" have, respectively, the meanings

set forth in section 101 (relating to definitions) of title 17 [17 USCS § 101]; and

(2) the terms "reproduction" and "distribution" refer to the exclusive rights of a copyright owner under clauses (1) and (3) respectively of section 106 (relating to exclusive rights in copyrighted works) [17 USCS § 106 (1), (3)], as limited by sections 107 through 118, of title 17 [17 USCS §§ 107–118].

(Added May 24, 1982, P. L. 97-180, § 3, 96 Stat. 92.)

Uniform Trade Secrets Act

(Adopted by the Commissioners on Uniform States Laws at their 1979 Annual Conference; adopted in various forms in fifteen states)

§ 1. [Definitions]

As used in this Act, unless the context requires otherwise:

(1) "Improper means" includes theft, bribery, misrepresentation, breach or inducement of a breach of a duty to maintain secrecy, and espionage through electronic or other means;

(2) "Misappropriation" means:

(i) acquisition of a trade secret of another by a person who knows or has reason to know that the trade secret was acquired by improper means; or

(ii) disclosure or use of a trade secret of another without express or implied consent by a person who

(A) used improper means to acquire knowledge of the trade secret; or

(B) at the time of disclosure or use, knew or had reason to know that his knowledge of the trade secret was

(I) derived from or through a person who had used improper means to acquire it;

(II) acquired under circumstances giving rise to a duty to maintain its secrecy or limit its use; or

(III) derived from or through a person who owed a duty to the person seeking relief to maintain its secrecy or limit its use; or

(C) before a material change of his [or her] position, knew or had reason to know that it was a trade secret and that knowledge of it had been acquired by accident or mistake.

(3) "Person" means an individual, corporation, business trust, estate, trust, partnership, association joint venture, government, governmental subdivision or agency, or any other legal or commercial entity.

(4) "Trade secret" means information, including a formula, pattern, compilation, program, device, method, technique, or process, that:

(i) derives independent economic value, present or potential, from not being generally known to, and not being readily ascertainable by proper means by, other persons who can obtain economic value from its disclosure or use, and

(ii) is the subject of efforts that are reasonable under the circumstances to maintain its secrecy.

§ 2. [Injunctive Relief]

(a) Actual or threatened misappropriation may be enjoined. Upon application to the court, an injunction must be terminated when the trade secret has ceased to exist, but the injunction may be continued for an additional reasonable period of time in order to eliminate commercial advantage that otherwise would be derived from the misappropriation.

(b) In exceptional circumstances, an injunction may condition future use upon payment of a reasonable royalty for no longer than the period of time for which use could have been prohibited. Exceptional circumstances include a material and prejudicial change of position before acquiring knowledge or reason to know of misappropriation that renders a prohibitive injunction inequitable.

(c) In appropriate circumstances, the court may order affirmative acts to protect a trade secret.

§ 3. [Damages]

(a) In addition to or in lieu of injunctive relief, a complainant may recover damages for the actual loss caused by misappropriation. A complainant also may recover for the unjust enrichment caused by misappropriation that is not taken into account in computing damages for actual loss.

(b) If willful and malicious misappropriation exists, the court may award exemplary damages in an amount not exceeding twice the award made under subsection (a).

§ 4. [Attorney's Fees]

If (i) a claim of misappropriation is made in bad faith, (ii) a motion to terminate an injunction is made or resisted in bad faith, or (iii) willful and malicious misappropriation exists, the court may award reasonable attorney's fees to the prevailing party.

§ 5. [Preservation of Secrecy]

In an action under this Act, the court shall preserve the secrecy of an alleged trade secret by reasonable means, which may include granting protective orders in connection with discovery proceedings, holding in-camera hearings, sealing the records of the action, and ordering any person involved in the litigation not to disclose an alleged trade secret without previous court approval.

§ 6. [Statute of Limitations]

An action for misappropriation must be brought within three years after the misappropriation is discovered or by the exercise of reasonable diligence should have been discovered. For the purposes of this section, a continuing misappropriation constitutes a single claim.

§ 7. [Effect on Other Law]

(a) Except as provided in subsection (b), this Act displaces conflicting tort, restitutionary, and other law of this State pertaining to civil remedies for misappropriation of a trade secret.

(b) This Act does not affect:

(1) contractual remedies, whether or not based upon misappropriation of a trade secret; or

(2) other civil remeddies that are not based upon misappropriation of a trade secret; or

(3) criminal sanctions, whether or not based upon misappropriation of a trade secret.

§ 8. [Uniformity of Application and Construction]

This Act shall be applied and construed to effectuate its general purpose to make uniform the law with respect to the subject of this Act among states enacting it.

§ 9. [Short Title]

This Act may be cited as the Uniform Trade Secrets Act.

§ 10. [Severability]

If any provision of this Act or its application to any person or circumstances is held invalid, the invalidity does not affect other provisions or applications of the Act which can be given effect without the invalid provision or application, and to this end the provisions of this Act are severable.

§ 11. [Time of Taking Effect]

This Act takes effect on _____ .

§ 12. [Repeal]

The following Acts and parts of Acts are repealed:

(1)

(2)
(3)

§ 13.   [Application to Existing Relationships]

This Act does not apply to a misappropriation that occurred before the effective date or to a misappropriation that began before and continues after the effective date.

The Uniform Trade Secrets Act has been adopted in the following states:

Jurisdiction	Laws	Effective Date	Statute Citation
California	1984, c.1724	1-1-85	West's Ann.Cal.Civ. Code §§ 3426 to 3426.10
Connecticut	1983, No. 344	6-23-83	(CGSA § 35-50 to 35-58)
Delaware	1982 (63 Del. Laws) c.218	4-15-82	6 Del. C. § 2001-2009 6 Del. C § 2001-2009
Idaho	1981, ch. 240		Bobbs Merrill Idaho Code 48-801 to 48-807.
Indiana	1982, No. 1257	2-25-82	West's A.I.C. 24-2-3-1 to 24-2-3-8
Kansas	1981, c. 214	7-1-81	K.S.A. 60-3320 to 60-3330
Louisiana	1981, No. 462	7-19-81	L.S.A.-R.S. 51:1431 to 51:1439
Minnesota	1980, ch. 594	1-1-81	M.S.A. § 325C.01 to 325C.08
Montana	1985, c. 104		MCA 30-14-401 to 30-14-409.
North Dakota	1983, c. 508	7-1-83	NDCC 47-25.1-01 to 47-25.1-08.
Oklahoma	1986, c. 85	11-1-86	78 O.S.A. SS 85 to 95
Virginia	1986, c. 210	7-1-86	Va. C. 1950, SS 59.1-336 to 59.1-343
Washington	1981, c. 286	1-1-82	West's R.C.W.A. 19.108.010 to 19.108.940
West Virginia	1986, c. 168	7-1-86	W.V.C. 47-22-1 to 47-22-10
Wisconsin	1985 Act 236, S 6	4-24-86	W.S.A. 134.90

Minnesota Uniform Trade Secrets Act
(Minnesota Statutes Annotated Sections 325C.01 to 325C.08)

325C.01   Definitions

Subdivision 1. As used in sections 325C.01 to 325C.07, the terms defined in these sections have the meanings given them, unless the context requires otherwise:

Subd. 2. "Improper means" includes theft, bribery, misrepresentation, breach or inducement of a breach of a duty to maintain secrecy, or espionage through electronic or other means;

Subd. 3. "Misappropriation" means:

(i) acquisition of a trade secret of another by a person who knows or has reason to know that the trade secret was acquired by improper means; or

(ii) disclosure or use of a trade secret of another without express or implied consent by the person who

(A) used improper means to acquire knowledge of the trade secret; or

(B) at the time of disclosure or use, knew or had reason to know that the discloser's or user's knowledge of the trade secret was

(I) derived from or through a person who had utilized improper means to acquire it;

(II) acquired under circumstances giving rise to a duty to maintain its secrecy or limit its use; or

(III) derived from or through a person who owed a duty to the person seeking relief to maintain its secrecy or limit its use; or

(C) before a material change of the discloser's or user's position, knew or had reason to know that it was a trade secret and that knowledge of it had been acquired by accident or mistake.

Subd. 4. "Person" means a natural person, corporation, business trust, estate, trust, partnership, association, joint venture, government, governmental subdivision or agency, or any other legal or commercial entity.

Subd. 5. "Trade secret" means information, including a formula, pattern, compilation, program, device, method, technique, or process, that:

(i) derives independent economic value, actual or potential, from not being generally known to, and not being readily ascertainable by proper means by, other persons who can obtain economic value from its disclosure or use, and

(ii) is the subject of efforts that are reasonable under the circumstances to maintain its secrecy.

The existence of a trade secret is not negated merely because an employee or other person has acquired the trade secret without express or specific notice that it is a trade secret if, under all the circumstances, the employee or other person knows or has reason to know that the owner intends or expects the secrecy of the type of information comprising the trade secret to be maintained.
Amended by Laws 1985, c. 196, § 1, eff. May 24, 1985; Laws 1986, c. 444.

325C.02 Injunctive relief

(a) Actual or threatened misappropriation may be enjoined. Upon application to the court, an injunction shall be terminated when the trade secret has ceased to exist, but the injunction may be continued for an additional reasonable period of time in order to eliminate commercial advantage that otherwise would be derived from the misappropriation.

(b) If the court determines that it would be unreasonable to prohibit future use, an injunction may condition future use upon payment of (1) an equitable royalty for no longer than the period of time the use could have been prohibited; or (2) other compensation.

(c) In appropriate circumstances, affirmative acts to protect a trade secret may be compelled by court order.
Laws 1980, c. 594, § 4, eff. Aug. 1, 1980.

325C.03 Damages

(a) In addition to or in lieu of injunctive relief, a complainant may recover damages for the actual loss caused by misappropriation. A complainant also may recover for the unjust enrichment caused by misappropriation that is not taken into account in computing damages for actual loss.

(b) If willful and malicious misappropriation exists, the court may award exemplary damages in an amount which the court deems just and equitable.
Laws 1980, c. 594, § 5, eff. Aug. 1, 1980.

325C.04 Attorney's fees

If (i) a claim of misappropriation is made in bad faith, (ii) a motion to terminate an injunction is made or resisted in bad faith, or (iii) willful and malicious misappropriation exists, the court may award reasonable attorney's fees to the prevailing party.
Laws 1980, c. 594, § 6, eff. Aug. 1, 1980.

325C.05 Preservation of secrecy

In an action under sections 325C.01 to 325C.07, a court shall preserve the secrecy of an alleged trade secret by reasonable means, which may include

granting protective orders in connection with discovery proceedings, holding in-camera hearings, sealing the records of the action, and ordering any person involved in the litigation not to disclose an alleged trade secret without prior court approval.
Laws 1980, c. 594, § 7, eff. Aug. 1, 1980.

325C.06   Statute of limitations

An action for misappropriation must be brought within three years after the misappropriation is discovered or by the exercise of reasonable diligence should have been discovered. For the purposes of this section, a continuing misappropriation constitutes a single claim.
Laws 1980, c. 594, § 8, eff. Aug. 1, 1980.

325C.07   Effect on other law

(a) Sections 325C.01 to 325C.07 displace conflicting tort, restitutionary, and other law of this state pertaining to civil liability for misappropriation of a trade secret.

(b) Sections 325C.01 to 325C.07 do not affect:

(1) contractual or other civil liability or relief that is not based upon misappropriation of a trade secret; or
(2) criminal liability for misappropriation of a trade secret.

Laws 1980, c. 594, § 9, eff. Aug. 1, 1980.

325C.08   Short title

Sections 325C.01 to 325C.07 may be cited as the "Uniform Trade Secrets Act."
Laws 1980, c. 594, § 10.

Restatement (First) of Torts Section 757

§ 757. Liability for Disclosure or Use of Another's Trade Secret—General Principle.

One who discloses or uses another's trade secret, without a privilege to do so, is liable to the other if

(a) he discovered the secret by improper means, or

(b) his disclosure or use constitutes a breach of confidence reposed in him by the other in disclosing the secret to him, or

(c) he learned the secret from a third person with notice of the facts that it was a secret and that the third person discovered it by improper means or that the third person's disclosure of it was otherwise a breach of his duty to the other, or

(d) he learned the secret with notice of the facts that it was a secret and that its disclosure was made to him by mistake.

Uniform Commercial Code, Section 2-103

UCC § 2-103. Definitions and Index of Definitions.

(1) In this Article unless the context otherwise requires

(a) "Buyer" means a person who buys or contracts to buy goods.
(b) "Good faith" in the case of a merchant means honesty in fact and the observance of reasonable commercial standards of fair dealing in the trade.
(c) "Receipt" of goods means taking physical possession of them.
(d) "Seller" means a person who sells or contracts to sell goods.

(2) Other definitions applying to this Article or to specified Parts thereof, and the sections in which they appear are:

> "Acceptance". Section 2-606.
> "Banker's credit". Section 2-325.
> "Between merchants". Section 2-104.
> "Cancellation". Section 2-106(4).
> "Commercial unit". Section 2-105.
> "Confirmed credit". Section 2-325.
> "Conforming to contract". Section 2-106.
> "Contract for sale". Section 2-106.
> "Cover". Section 2-712.
> "Entrusting". Section 2-403.
> "Financing agency". Section 2-104.
> "Future goods". Section 2-105.
> "Goods". Section 2-105.
> "Identification". Section 2-501.
> "Installment contract". Section 2-612.
> "Letter of Credit". Section 2-325.
> "Lot". Section 2-105.
> "Merchant". Section 2-104.
> "Overseas". Section 2-323.
> "Person in position of seller. Section 2-707.
> "Present sale". Section 2-106.
> "Sale". Section 2-106.
> "Sale on approval". Section 2-326.
> "Sale or return". Section 2-326.
> "Termination". Section § 2-106.

(3) The following definitions in other Articles apply to this Article:

> "Check". Section 3-104.
> "Consignee". Section 7-102.
> "Consignor". Section 7-102.
> "Consumer goods". Section 9-109.

"Dishonor". Section 3-507.

"Draft". Section 3-104.

(4) In addition Article 1 contains general definitions and principles of construction and interpretation applicable throughout this Article.

Uniform Commercial Code Section 2-302

UCC § 2-302. Unconscionable Contract or Clause.

(1) If the court as a matter of law finds the contract or any clause of the contract to have been unconscionable at the time it was made the court may refuse to enforce the contract, or it may enforce the remainder of the contract without the unconscionable clause, or it may so limit the application of any unconscionable clause as to avoid any unconscionable result.

(2) When it is claimed or appears to the court that the contract or any clause thereof may be unconscionable the parties shall be afforded a reasonable opportunity to present evidence as to its commercial setting, purpose and effect to aid the court in making the determination.

Restatement (Second) of Contracts Section 208

§ 208. Unconscionable Contract or Term

If a contract or term thereof is unconscionable at the time the contract is made a court may refuse to enforce the contract, or may enforce the remainder of the contract without the unconscionable term, or may so limit the application of any unconscionable term as to avoid any unconscionable result.

California Civil Code Section 1670.5

§ 1670.5. Unconscionable contract or clause of contract; finding as matter of law; remedies

(a) If the court as a matter of law finds the contract or any clause of the contract to have been unconscionable at the time it was made the court may refuse to enforce the contract, or it may enforce the remainder of the contract without the unconscionable clause, or it may so limit the application of any unconscionable clause as to avoid any unconscionable result.

(b) When it is claimed or appears to the court that the contract or any clause thereof may be unconscionable the parties shall be afforded a reasonable opportunity to present evidence as to its commercial setting, purpose, and effect to aid the court in making the determination.
(Added by Stats. 1979, c. 819, p. 2827, § 3, urgency, eff. Sept. 19, 1979.)

California Business & Professions Code Section 16600

§ 16600. Invalidity of contracts.

Except as provided in this chapter, every contract by which anyone is restrained from engaging in a lawful profession, trade, or business of any kind is to that extent void.
(Added Stats. 1941, c. 526, § 1.)

California Labor Code Section 2860

§ 2860. Ownership of things acquired by virtue of employment

Everything which an employee acquires by virtue of his employment, except the compensation which is due to him from his employer, belongs to the employer, whether acquired lawfully or unlawfully, or during or after the expiration of the term of his employment.
(Stats. 1937, c. 90, p. 260, § 2860.)

California Labor Code Sections 2870 through 2872

§ 2870. Employment agreements; assignment of rights

(a) Any provision in an employment agreement which provides that an employee shall assign, or offer to assign, any of his or her rights in an invention to his or her employer shall not apply to an invention that the employee developed entirely on his or her own time without using the employers' equipment, supplies, facilities, or trade secret information except for those inventions that either:

(1) Relate at the time of conception or reduction to practice of the invention to the employer's business, or actual or demonstrably anticipated research or development of the employer.
(2) Result from any work performed by the employee for the employer.

(b) To the extent a provision in an employment agreement purports to require an employee to assign an invention otherwise excluded from being required to be assigned under subdivision (a), the provision is * * * against the public policy of this state and * * * is unenforceable.
(Added by Stats.1979, c. 1001, p. 3401, § 1. Amended by Stats.1986, c. 346, § 1.)

§ 2871. Conditions of employment or continued employment; disclosure of inventions

No employer shall require a provision made void and unenforceable by Section 2870 as a condition of employment or continued employment. Nothing in this article shall be construed to forbid or restrict the right of an employer to provide in contracts of employment for disclosure, provided that any such disclosures be received in confidence, of all of the employee's

inventions made solely or jointly with others during the term of his or her employment, a review process by the employer to determine such issues as may arise, and for full title to certain patents and inventions to be in the United States, as required by contracts between the employer and the United States or any of its agencies.
(Added by Stats.1979, c. 1001, p. 3401, § 1.)

§ 2872.   Notice to employee; burden of proof

If an employment agreement entered into after January 1, 1980, contains a provision requiring the employee to assign or offer to assign any of his or her rights in any invention to his or her employer, the employer must also, at the time the agreement is made, provide a written notification to the employee that the agreement does not apply to an invention which qualifies fully under the provisions of Section 2870. In any suit or action arising thereunder, the burden of proof shall be on the employee claiming the benefits of its provisions.
(Added by Stats.1979, c. 1001, p. 3401, § 1.)

Minnesota Statutes Annotated Section 181.78

181.78. Agreements; terms relating to inventions

Subdivision 1. Any provision in an employment agreement which provides that an employee shall assign or offer to assign any of his rights in an invention to his employer shall not apply to an invention for which no equipment, supplies, facility or trade secret information of the employer was used and which was developed entirely on the employee's own time, and (1) which does not relate (a) directly to the business of the employer or (b) to the employer's actual or demonstrably anticipated research or development, or (2) which does not result from any work performed by the employee for the employer. Any provision which purports to apply to such an invention is to that extent against the public policy of this state and is to that extent void and unenforceable.

Subd. 2. No employer shall require a provision made void and unenforceable by subdivision 1 as a condition of employment or continuing employment.

Subd. 3. If an employment agreement entered into after August 1, 1977, contains a provision requiring the employee to assign or offer to assign any of the employee's rights in any invention to an employer, the employer must also, at the time the agreement is made, provide a written notification to the employee that the agreement does not apply to an invention for which no equipment, supplies, facility or trade secret information of the employer was used and which was developed entirely on the employee's own time, and (1) which does not relate (a) directly to the business of the employer or (b) to the employer's actual or demonstrably anticipated research or development, or (2) which does not result from any work performed by the employee for the employer.
Laws 1977, c. 47 § 1. Amended by Laws 1986, c. 444.

Washington Revised Code Sections
49.44.140 to 49.44.150

49.44.140. Requiring assignment of employee's rights to inventions—Conditions

(1) A provision in an employment agreement which provides that an employee shall assign or offer to assign any of the employee's rights in an invention to the employer does not apply to an invention for which no equipment, supplies, facilities, or trade secret information of the employer was used and which was developed entirely on the employee's own time, unless (a) the invention relates (i) directly to the business of the employer, or (ii) to the employer's actual or demonstrably anticipated research or development, or (b) the invention results from any work performed by the employee for the employer. Any provision which purports to apply to such an invention is to that extent against the public policy of this state and is to that extent void and unenforceable.

(2) An employer shall not require a provision made void and unenforceable by subsection (1) of this section as a condition of employment or continuing employment.

(3) If an employment agreement entered into after September 1, 1979, contains a provision requiring the employee to assign any of the employee's rights in any invention to the employer, the employer must also, at the time the agreement is made, provide a written notification to the employee that the agreement does not apply to an invention for which no equipment, supplies, facility, or trade secret information of the employer was used and which was developed entirely on the employee's own time, unless (a) the invention relates (i) directly to the business of the employer, or (ii) to the employer's actual or demonstrably anticipated research or development, or (b) the invention results from any work performed by the employee for the employer.
Added by Laws 1979, Ex.Sess., ch. 177, § 2, eff. Sept. 1, 1979.

49.44.150. Requiring assignment of employee's rights to inventions—Disclosure of inventions by employee

Even though the employee meets the burden of proving the conditions specified in RCW 49.44.140, the employee shall, at the time of employment or thereafter, disclose all inventions being developed by the employee, for the purpose of determining employer or employee rights. The employer or the employee may disclose such inventions to the department of employment security, and the department shall maintain a record of such disclosures for a minimum period of five years.
Added by Laws 1979, Ex.Sess., ch. 177, § 3, eff. Sept. 1, 1979.

Table of Cases

Index